Teaching Ethics:
Care, Think and Choose

A curriculum-based approach to ethical thinking

by
Paul Jewell
Pauline Webster
Lesley Henderson
Jill Dodd
Sonja Paterson
Jill McLaughlin

Hawker Brownlow
EDUCATION

Published in Australia by

Hawker Brownlow
EDUCATION

P.O. Box 580, Moorabbin, Victoria 3189, Australia
Phone: (03) 8558 2444 Fax: (03) 8558 2400
Toll Free Ph: 1800 334 603 Fax: 1800 150 445
Website: *www.hbe.com.au*
Email: *orders@hbe.com.au*

Code: HB2547
ISBN: 978 1 74239 254 7
0711

Printed in Australia

Contents

© 2011 Hawker Brownlow Education • 9781742392547 • HB2547

© 2011 Hawker Brownlow Education • 9781742392547 • HB2547

Chapter 1
How to use this book

This chapter provides:

- a rationale for the teaching of ethics

- a description of four strategies for ethical decision-making

- an overview of the book's chapters

- Resource Sheet: Four ways of thinking about ethics

This book provides a means of teaching ethics throughout the curriculum, through the integration of ethical questions in the teaching of English, society and environment, drama and mathematics. It is written by practising classroom teachers who have studied ethics formally. The various chapters provide practical classroom techniques and explanations of ethical strategies. While the book is aimed at the middle school level, the strategies outlined can be easily adapted for other levels.

The first three chapters discuss the nature of ethics, reasons for teaching ethics and methods of teaching: the *why*, the *what* and the *how*. Chapter One provides an overview of the material within the book, and Chapter Two presents a method of teaching ethics. Chapter Three provides a moral reasoning method. These chapters provide an introduction to the ideas recurring in the following chapters, which apply ethics to various areas of the curriculum such as drama, or society and environment. Thus, Chapters One to Three should be read in conjunction with the ensuing chapters.

Why teach ethics in the classroom?

It is a fact of life that people need to learn how to get along with each other, and the success of any community depends upon how well its members achieve this. The lifelong happiness and success of any individual depends upon how well that person develops dispositions and strategies that enable them to get along with others. In the school setting, children learn how to deal with others. They learn from each other, from their teachers and from the way the school is organised. Their learning may be haphazard, incorporating a random mix of good and bad strategies, or their teachers may make a conscious effort to instil worthwhile and positive social behaviours.

For the purposes of this book, ethics is defined as the study of how people should treat each other. No distinction is made between the words 'ethical' and 'moral'. The authors recognise that contemporary society is characterised by rapid change, and that a citizenry that is democratic and well-educated is best placed to cope with these changes. Well-educated people can discuss how to treat each other, negotiating agreed outcomes when confronting technical, social and ethical challenges.

What are ethical decisions?

Whenever people make decisions involving choices between right and wrong, good or bad, or people's welfare and interests, they are making ethical decisions. When they make recommendations, when they use words like 'ought' or 'should', they are asking others to make ethical decisions. Sound ethical decision-making characteristically combines higher-order critical thinking skills with empathy. Ethics has both cognitive and affective dimensions.

Establishing an ethical climate

This book's focus is introducing and equipping students with the tools to help them make ethical decisions. No book, by itself, will dissuade people who are inclined to do the wrong thing. Instructing students that copying another's work is against the rules, for example, will not ensure that lazy students make the effort to produce their own work. Aristotle, one of the first philosophers to write about ethics, said that a good choice is the result of sound reasoning and right desire. Both are necessary. The desire to do the right thing can be stimulated by the right sort of community and classroom climate. The components of a positive ethical climate include:

- discipline aimed at helping children become self-disciplined and willing to take responsibility for their own actions
- communication which is open and respectful
- family support and a responsive learning environment
- attitudes and examples by teachers and peers that reflect values such as justice, cooperation and respect for others
- teaching behaviours that aim to develop the child's positive self-esteem.

While good intentions are necessary for ethical action, they are not sufficient in themselves. If people want to do the right thing, they need to know how to decide what the right thing is.

How to teach ethics using four ethical strategies

Ethics, a study in its own right, is part of philosophy. Some useful ideas drawn from philosophical ethics are summarised in the table, 'Four ways of thinking about ethics'. The 'Four ways of thinking about ethics' are applied to each curriculum area in the ensuing chapters. They serve as strategies for making decisions and negotiating ethical agreements with others.

The four strategies involve consideration of:

- principles
- consequences
- agreements, and
- virtues.

Principles

Principles are like duties or rules. They are the guiding standards for leading a moral life. Principles are universally applicable, meaning that they apply to any set of circumstances. So, for example, if I argue that it is never right to tell a lie, I am appealing to principle. When

© 2011 Hawker Brownlow Education • 9781742392547 • HB2547

using the strategy of appealing to principle, I am deciding to do something because it is the right thing, rather than the expedient thing, to do. Principles are very useful for dealing with large groups of people. Many laws are based on principles agreed to by lawmakers and, it is assumed, by the rest of society. Some common principles are:

- Always tell the truth.

- Keep your promises.

- Be fair.

- Respect human life.

- Don't use people. Always treat others as ends in themselves, not as a means to your own ends.

This leads to the principle of respecting the rights of the individual. The right to freedom, the right to free speech and the right to equal treatment are ethical principles. One well-known fundamental principle is the Golden Rule: 'Treat others as you would want them to treat you.'

Consequences

All actions and decisions have consequences. What makes an action right is whether it has good consequences, such as whether it increases the welfare of the people affected by it. If a large number of people are affected, the greatest good for the greatest number might become a consideration. 'Good' might mean happiness, well-being, pleasure, interest or satisfaction. When considering consequences, the possible benefits of an action need to be weighed against potentially negative results. Whether or not all the possible consequences are known is not, however, an ethical problem, but a practical one. Ethical decisions can only be made with reference to known consequences.

Agreements

A good way to decide the best way to treat people is to ask them how they want to be treated. People can then reach agreements about how to treat each other. Agreements have a great deal of ethical power, because human beings are more likely to adhere to something they have agreed to, rather than conform to something that has been imposed on them. This is how contracts work, which is why 'agreement' in this sense is sometimes called a social contract. A social contract is an agreement between citizens about the sort of society in which they wish to live. Democracy is an example of a social contract at work.

Virtues

Virtues are character traits. A virtuous person does the right thing out of habit. To put it the other way around, the right thing to do is what a virtuous person would do. Some commonly recognised virtues are integrity, courage and compassion.

Combining the four strategies and resolving dilemmas

Usually, these four strategies provide clear guidelines for ethical decision-making, whether acting as a citizen, individual, adult or student. Should I steal my classmate's pocket money? No, because stealing is wrong in principle and causes harm to others. Should I stick up for my friend who is being teased, or join in the teasing? I should act courageously and support my friend. Sometimes, however, the right decision is not so clear. Perhaps sticking to principles will bring about bad consequences. Perhaps caring about another's welfare will involve me in a mess of lies and compromise my integrity. Or perhaps the agreements being proposed by my community seem wrong to me. Circumstances like these require a careful combining and balancing of the four strategies.

A person considering an ethical question can use one or a combination of these strategies. In an ideal world, a solution would satisfy all four. A virtuous person could act according to that principle that was agreed would be most likely to increase everyone's well-being. In the real world, however, people often face dilemmas caused by a conflict of strategies. Resolving such dilemmas can be regarded as ethical budgeting. The perfect solution might not be possible, but some decisions are better than others. In the real world, too, people do not make decisions in isolation. Other people are inevitably involved. The four strategies provide a means for people to confer, to explain their positions and to co-operate effectively.

Using this book to apply the four strategies within the curriculum

To make discussions about ethics fruitful, a classroom culture of reasonable behaviour should be established. A group of people who exchange views reasonably, with the common aim of collectively coming to the best decision, is called a 'Community of Inquiry'.

Establishing and running this community is the subject of the next chapter, 'Getting students to discuss and decide: How to conduct a Community of Inquiry Session'.

In Chapter Three, 'PAVE: The way to developing sound moral reasoning across the curriculum', we show how ethics can be infused into the curriculum by providing methods to apply reasoning strategies for a variety of issues.

In Chapter Four, 'Ethical decision-making through stories', reasoning strategies are applied to stories.

Practising classroom inquiry is based upon tales, some of which are well known, while others are fresh and thought provoking. The difference between the presentation of facts and ethical judgements is then discussed in Chapter Five, 'Using statistics in ethical decision-making'.

Drama can provide excellent opportunities for the identification and communication of differing views, through role-play and the expression of character. This is explored in Chapter Six, 'Walking in another's shoes: Active listening and role-play in drama'.

Chapter Seven, 'Off the classroom wall and out into the world – Moving from static projects to active citizenship in society and environment programs' explains how to enable students to examine the role of the individual in society.

Chapter Eight provides tools for evaluating development in moral reasoning.

The fascination of ethics

Our task as teachers is to inspire in our students the belief that the ethical life is a worthwhile pursuit, as well as a fascinating challenge to their cognitive and emotional characters. We wish to empower students with the knowledge, skills and dispositions that will enable them to make well-reasoned ethical decisions, which will result in making the world a better place.

© 2011 Hawker Brownlow Education • 9781742392547 • HB2547

Four ways of thinking about ethics

Principles

Principles are like duties or rules that apply to any set of circumstances. So, for example, when we argue that it is never right to tell a lie, we are thinking about principles. Principles are useful for dealing with large groups of people. Many laws are based on principles. Some common principles are: Always tell the truth. Keep your promises. Be fair. Respect others' rights.

Consequences

What makes an action right is whether it has good consequences. That is, whether it increases the welfare of those affected by it. If large numbers of people are affected, we might try to consider the greatest good for the greatest number. By 'good', we might mean happiness, well-being, pleasure, interest or satisfaction.

Agreements

A good way to decide the best way to treat people is to ask them how they want to be treated. People can then come to agreements about how to treat each other. A group of friends might agree to play sport on Saturdays, or a community might make laws.

Virtues

Virtues are character traits. A virtuous person does the right thing out of habit. To put it the other way around, the right thing to do is what a virtuous person would do. Some commonly recognised virtues are integrity, courage and compassion.

Chapter 2

Getting students to discuss and decide: How to conduct Community of Inquiry sessions

This chapter provides:

- a rationale of how and why to conduct a Community of Inquiry

- a lesson plan for a typical Community of Inquiry

- a list of some advantages of a Community of Inquiry

- Resource Sheets:

    Four things a reasonable person knows

    Code of Conduct for a Community of Inquiry

    Discussion ideas for a Community of Inquiry

While twentieth-century education focused on the acquisition of knowledge and skills, teachers in the twenty-first century also seek wisdom for their students, and for themselves. We acknowledge that individual leaders cannot solve global problems, and recognise that each one of us has an integral role to play in confronting problems concerning the environment, economic inequality and racial conflict. Therefore, we all need to be effective at thinking, listening and conferring. We need to have the skills to exchange views reasonably, with the common aim of collectively coming to the best possible decision. Community of Inquiry trains us to do just this.

Members of a Community of Inquiry admit their fallibility

For there to be a fruitful exchange of views, reasonable people realise that they are fallible, and so listen productively to other viewpoints. One of the most productive techniques available to reasonable people is to present their ideas and invite criticism. This technique, however, can be psychologically difficult. It is not easy to display weakness or admit to being wrong. Reasonable people overcome this difficulty by practising the following precepts.

Four things a reasonable person knows

1. I don't understand my own point of view unless I understand those opposing it.

2. I don't understand opposing viewpoints until I can state them so well that those who hold them agree with my summary.

3. Some of the things I believe in firmly are, undoubtedly, absolutely wrong.

4. If I am not willing to change my mind, I am not a reasonable person.

What are we trying to do in a Community of Inquiry?

A Community of Inquiry explores a question, problem or issue that doesn't have a straightforward answer that can be found somewhere. The answer to 'What is magnetism?' can readily be found. But questions such as 'Should we clone animals?' or 'Could a machine think?' don't have clear and immediate answers. These sorts of questions are grist for Community of Inquiry.

Some open questions are factual questions, and some are moral questions. 'Are dolphins as smart as humans?' and, 'Is it wrong to keep canaries in cages?' are both open questions. It is not the case that all factual questions are closed and all moral questions are open. A question is open if it provokes thought and discussion. In a Community of Inquiry, ideas are proposed, attacked, defended and examined for their strengths and weaknesses. But only the ideas are considered, not the individuals who propose them. A Community of Inquiry member might, for instance, propose an idea for discussion without personally subscribing to that idea. A Community of Inquiry is intellectually challenging, but personally safe. Its members adhere to a Code of Conduct.

Code of Conduct for Students Taking Part in a Community of Inquiry

1. Consider the idea not the person.

Avoid supporting or criticising an idea simply because it was presented by someone you like or dislike.

Do not try to beat the other person in an argument.

If your own idea is criticised, don't take it personally.

2. When you present an idea, invite critical assessment of it.

Say, for example:
'What do you think of what I just said?'
'Do you see any flaws in my reasoning?'
'Here's something I'm not too sure of ...'

3. Be a good listener.

Listen carefully to others' ideas.

Listen actively to others' ideas. Ask questions.

When someone says something with which you disagree, ask:
'How did you arrive at this position?'
'You may be right. I'd like to understand more.'
'What leads you to say ... ?'

And make sure you really understand the view presented:
'Am I correct that you are saying ... ?'

Listen empathetically. Try to see the idea from the speaker's perspective. Listen generously. Look for ways in which an idea moves the discussion forward. Listen critically. Look for flaws in the person's reasoning and for gaps in the speaker's knowledge, and try to think of alternative positions. But do not nitpick or become distracted by trivia.

4. Use the tools of clear thinking.

Follow the rules of logic that help to distinguish good arguments from bad.
Identify assumptions, opinions and bias.
Look for relationships between ideas that will lead to conclusions and generalisations.

Be careful about the language you use. For example, be careful that you do not over-generalise.

5. Seek to move the discussion towards a good resolution.

Try to move from simply sharing anecdotes and opinions to establishing criteria and finding justifiable answers and solutions.

Be prepared to change your mind. Review and reappraise your own ideas in the light of the discussion.

6. Don't sacrifice reaching a good conclusion because of time limits.

Be patient and willing to take the time to discuss an issue or idea until you arrive at a conclusion that everyone finds satisfactory, or a decision that will produce the most good. Be prepared to pause the discussion to find out something the group needs to know before proceeding further.

We recommend that classes practise this code. Teachers can introduce the code by presenting an open proposition and asking students to choose a number between 0 and 10 according to how closely they agree with the proposition. They could physically adopt a position by standing in a line relative to other members, or they could write their names somewhere where all can see. Once positions are known, the class can discuss the differences, exchange views and attempt to move towards an agreement.

In the Resource Sheets section at the end of this chapter, some discussion ideas for a Community of Inquiry are presented. These are open questions that teachers can use to teach their students about how to exchange views, before progressing to more sensitive ethical issues. Of course, there are many more possible discussion topics, and teachers should encourage their students to suggest ideas derived from their own interests.

A lesson plan for a Community of Inquiry Session

1. Resources

Provide students with the following Resource Sheets:

- Four things a reasonable person knows (p. 18)
- Code of Conduct for a Community of Inquiry (p. 19)
- Discussion ideas for a Community of Inquiry (p. 20)

'Four things a reasonable person knows' and 'Code of Conduct for a Community of Inquiry' can usefully be made into posters that hang permanently in the classroom.

 © 2011 Hawker Brownlow Education • 9781742392547 • HB2547

2. Discussion ideas sheet

Students tick 0 to 10 on their discussion ideas sheet to record their own views. They may ask for clarification of any ambiguities in the proposed ideas to be discussed, but they are not to argue them. Or, if necessary, clarification of ambiguities could be a task for community discussion. Students are to make up their own minds about the meaning of the ideas and their responses.

3. Paired discussion

After completing the discussion ideas sheet, students discuss their positions with their immediate neighbour.

4. Establishing the code of behaviour for the discussion

The teacher explains the 'four things a reasonable person knows' and the 'Code of Conduct for a Community of Inquiry'.

5. Stating initial positions

Students share their positions regarding the discussion ideas with the rest of the class. This can be done on a blackboard/whiteboard, or more permanently on a large sheet of durable paper that can be preserved for future discussion. Students write their names on the board/card in the corresponding area to where they ticked their positions on their discussion ideas sheet. A spread of positions is expected.

6. Beginning discussion

A volunteer is asked to choose one of the items for discussion. The teacher chooses a student, identifies that student's position and asks the student to choose another student whose position is different. The two students are then asked to explain their positions to each other, and their reasons for holding them.

7. Involving others

The teacher invites contributions from the rest of the class. The formalities will vary from teacher to teacher and from class to class. Some teachers will require all statements to be preceded by a raised hand and permission to speak, while others will allow a free flow of ideas and comments. It can be beneficial to begin formally, and then move to a more informal expression of ideas. The teacher makes space in the discussion for the less forceful student, and rewards and encourages contribution.

8. Facilitating discussion

The teacher is not actually a member of the Community of Inquiry, but its 'executive secretary' or 'non-voting chair'. This is necessary because a Community of Inquiry is made up of equally empowered members, who are exchanging views with the aim of approaching agreement. Severe inequality, such as the teacher–student relationship, impairs this process and encourages the students to try to guess the 'correct' answer – that is, the teacher's views. In a Community of Inquiry, the community attempts to determine the best answer through its process of inquiry.

9. Resolving ambiguity

Students' positions may differ because they interpret terms differently. When discussing, for example, the statement 'dolphins are as smart as humans', it is up to the community to agree on a definition of the term 'smart' for the purposes of discussion. More than one definition may be considered, so that the community may agree that if smart means able to learn, then dolphins are smart, but if it means they can invent things, then they are not.

10. Reaffirming the code of behaviour

The behaviour in 'four things a reasonable person knows' and 'Code of Conduct for a Community of Inquiry' should be constantly referred to, required and practised.

11. Changing, explaining and justifying positions

Individual students may be asked to practise the second of the 'four things a reasonable person knows' by explaining positions they do not hold to their colleagues who do hold them, to ensure that there is mutual understanding. Positions that rely on claims of fact, such as whether dolphins use language, can be researched and reported back at a later stage. Students are encouraged to change their positions at any time, and as frequently as they wish.

12. Approaching agreement, or recognising intractable problems

One definition of 'truth' is that which would be arrived at by a group made up of reasonable and fully informed members. Periodically, the teacher should summarise the discussion's progress, identifying sticking points and ways to overcome them. Consensus may be reached. If not, progress towards it should be noted, as well as the obstacles that could not be overcome. A discussion should be wound up before it becomes tedious. The Community of Inquiry may dissolve, or it may move on to discuss a different idea.

13. Maintaining inquiry

Once students are familiar with the practice, the teacher can decide whether to run a Community of Inquiry as a stand-alone lesson, to apply it whenever useful, or to expect it as a continuous approach to learning and classroom behaviour.

Some advantages of a Community of Inquiry

- Students engaged in a Community of Inquiry gain the skills of dialogue and flexible thinking essential in contemporary society. These students are not trying to convince others to adopt their positions. They throw their ideas into a communal pool, from which they hope to draw insight and new possibilities. They are prepared to seriously listen and to consider other points of view. When they draw conclusions and make decisions, they realise that these are always tentative because they are based only on current knowledge and insight, which may change later. Community of Inquiry develops dispositions such as flexibility and tolerance of ambiguity.

- Community of Inquiry builds a sense of trust, cooperation and civility within classrooms. The aim of discussion is to find the truth, or to discern what ought to happen. As participants engage in personal and collective inquiry, considerable trust and ownership develops. As individuals reveal their uncertainties and genuinely seek feedback from others, barriers of hostility and mistrust are broken down. All ideas are valued and carefully considered. Participants prevent the discussion from swerving towards a contest between personalities. Unlike class meetings, majority vote is avoided. Instead, a result

© 2011 Hawker Brownlow Education • 9781742392547 • HB2547

that offers the most positive outcome for all is sought. Participants weigh the various degrees of impact upon individuals or groups, and consider the future impact of actions.

People are more likely to care about an issue after participating in Community of Inquiry for several reasons:

- They have carefully analysed the issue and made sense of it for themselves. Often, teachers segment an inquiry into several sessions to give students time to reflect on what has been said, or to conduct further research and investigation. Self-direction is an important feature of Community of Inquiry.

- They have had the opportunity to openly express, and examine, their own thoughts and feelings, no matter how seriously they clashed with others. In fact, others in the group were actually pleased that they offered a different perspective. They showed respect and took all ideas seriously. Encouraged by others, individuals flex the parameters of their beliefs and reasoning. This self-correction would not happen as readily if students had not felt that their ideas mattered and were taken seriously.

- The very nature of inquiry demands a certain degree of responsibility. The inquirers first ask, 'What is happening here?' This then leads to, 'What should be happening?' and subsequently to, 'What should I, or we, do about this?'

Community of Inquiry is a potent tool for developing empathy and caring thinking, and it is the contemporary mode of classroom discourse. It prefers dialogue to debate. It recognises the interdependence of individuals for whom unity is secured through diversity, and through the blending of different perspectives and ideas. Because participants use tools of clear thinking, and because there is a concerted effort to find the truth, Community of Inquiry is not just a gabfest. Rather, it is a powerful vehicle for intellectual and ethical deliberation. Community of Inquiry is a significant means whereby teachers can nurture ethical, analytical, independent critical thinkers and active citizens.

Four things a reasonable person knows

1. I don't understand my own point of view unless I understand those opposing it.

2. I don't understand opposing viewpoints until I can state them so well that those who hold them agree with my summary.

3. Some of the things I firmly believe in are, undoubtedly, absolutely wrong.

4. If I am not willing to change my mind, I am not a reasonable person.

© 2011 Hawker Brownlow Education • 9781742392547 • HB2547

Code of Conduct for a Community of Inquiry

1. Consider the idea, not the person.

Avoid supporting or criticising an idea simply because it was presented by someone you like or dislike.
Do not try to beat the other person in an argument.
If your own idea is criticised, don't take it personally.

2. When you present an idea, invite critical assessment of it.

Say: 'What do you think of what I just said?'
'Do you see any flaws in my reasoning?'
'Here's something I'm not too sure of ...'

3. Be a good listener.

Listen carefully and actively to others' ideas. Ask questions, such as
'Am I correct that you are saying ... ?'
Listen generously: look for ways in which an idea moves the discussion forward.
Listen critically: look for strengths and flaws in the person's reasoning. Try to think of alternative positions.
Do not nitpick or become distracted by trivia.

4. Use the tools of clear thinking.

Follow the rules of logic that help to distinguish good arguments from bad.
Identify assumptions, opinions and bias.

5. Try to move the discussion to a good resolution.

Be prepared to change your mind.
Review and reappraise your own ideas in the light of the discussion.

6. Don't sacrifice reaching a good conclusion because of time limits.

Be patient and willing to take the time to discuss an issue or idea until you arrive at a conclusion that everyone finds satisfactory, or a decision that will produce the most good.

Discussion ideas for a Community of Inquiry

Tick a position (0 to 10) alongside each of the ideas listed, saying how likely you think it is that the statement is true. Compare responses with your classmates. Then make a list of other statements you think would produce interesting discussion.

very unlikely very likely	
0 ... 1 ... 2 ... 3 ... 4 ... 5 ... 6 ... 7 ... 8 ... 9 ... 10	
	You can be anything you want if you try hard enough.
	Talents are inherited.
	One day people will learn to live in peace.
	Dolphins are as smart as humans.
	Soon we will be able to build a thinking machine.
	There is life after death.
	Telepathy can happen.
	Everest is the tallest mountain in the world.
	Fast food is bad for you.
	Aliens visit Earth.

 © 2011 Hawker Brownlow Education • 9781742392547 • HB2547

Chapter 3
PAVE: The way to developing sound moral reasoning through the curriculum

This chapter provides:

- a rationale for teaching moral reasoning
- a description of four strategies for ethical decision-making
- stepping through the PAVE strategy: a teaching plan
- Resource Sheets:

  PAVE moral reasoning strategy

  Question starters

  PAVE strategy

  Principles

  Agreements

  Virtues

  End consequences

  Reflection journal ideas

Please note: Chapters One and Two provide essential material on the conduct of ethical decision-making, and should be read in conjunction with this chapter. Chapter Eight provides evaluation and assessment tools.

In Chapter One, we introduced four ethical strategies that are commonly used in moral philosophy (see the Resource Sheet on page 11). In this chapter, we incorporate these strategies into a procedure of ethical decision-making, referred to as the PAVE moral reasoning strategy. The letters PAVE each represent one of those four ways of thinking about ethics.

- Principles
- Agreements
- Virtues
- End consequences.

A rationale for teaching moral reasoning

Teaching reasoning strategies in the context of a relevant situation is integral to the process of teaching. Reasoning strategies are acquired developmentally, since 'thinking is always an adaptive process in which the thinker must be able to utilise his or her current knowledge base to deal with new and novel situations that call for some decision or action' (Feldhusen, 1989). The aim of teaching thinking strategies and applying them to issues of a moral nature is to develop thoughtful students who are both effective and affective thinkers. This chapter presents a moral reasoning strategy that can be applied to solving moral dilemmas in all subject areas and at all age levels.

What is moral reasoning?

Whenever a question arises that involves the choice between right or wrong, good or bad, our own or others' well-being, it is a moral issue. Moral reasoning is the application of higher-order critical thinking skills, combined with caring thinking skills, to solve problems of a moral nature. There are both cognitive and affective aspects to moral reasoning. The cognitive skills of metacognition, logical-rational evaluation, critical-analytical thinking and problem solving work together with the affective abilities of empathy, openness, trust and tolerance. This combination of intellectual learning with the moral dimension can be referred to as 'wider order thinking' (Folsom, 1989:256).

What is the connection between intelligence and moral reasoning?

The ability to reason well is central to the concept of intelligence, but intelligence alone will not guarantee morality. To recognise the 'right' choice, and to judge our own and others' actions, is to make an act of reason. To choose to value morality and to make the 'right' choice is an act of character. The link between intelligence and choice 'makes the whole idea of morality possible in the first place [...] that's ultimately why we hold people responsible for what they do, because their intelligence gives them the power to choose how they'll behave' (Feldhusen, 1989).

High levels of cognitive intelligence and affective intelligence lead to the development of character, and ultimately to the potential for moral vision. The thinking, feeling person, in whom intelligence and character combine, can achieve the highest level of human development: self-actualisation. It is the confluence between cognitive intelligence, affective intelligence and the disposition towards morality that can determine an individual's moral reasoning ability. The greater the confluence between the three, the greater the individual's capacity to reason and behave morally. Without the disposition towards morality, the individual lacks the motivation for moral action.

Context is also an important consideration. Environmental, social, personal and situational contexts all influence an individual's choice to use reason and/or to behave morally. For example, an individual who is struggling to meet their basic needs may not consider the morality of whether or not to be opportunistic and take money from another person's wallet found on the ground, or whether to hand the wallet to the police. This relationship between cognitive intelligence, affective intelligence and personality, in context, and how this confluence influences an individual's moral reasoning and moral behaviour, is represented in the following graphic.

Context:

environmental

social

personal

situational

Cognitive intelligence

Affective intelligence

Moral reasoning and behaviour

Disposition towards morality

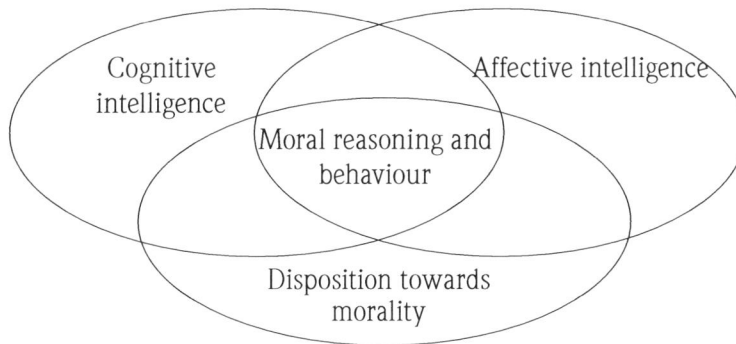

Why use moral dilemmas to encourage moral development?

Many theories of moral development describe the transition to higher stages of development occurring through the arousal of inner conflict (Piaget, 1965; Kohlberg, 1966; Dabrowski, 1964; Gilligan, 1982; Rest et al., 2000). It would seem that, just as a grain of sand causes the oyster to produce a pearl, the individual needs to experience a degree of inner friction or 'disequilibrium' to advance to higher levels of development (Piaget). Under the guidance of a perceptive and thoughtful teacher, the verbal conflict aroused through the consideration and discussion of a moral dilemma can create the desired stimulation.

Reasoning strategies are best learnt in the context of content that is relevant to the subject and to the students being taught. Moral dilemmas can be found in all curriculum subjects. Whenever an issue prompts the question 'What should I do?', and there are several justifiable alternatives with different outcomes, a moral dilemma is presented. The discussion of moral dilemmas actively involves the students in the process of decision-making, and demands a personal commitment to the choice. Rather than expecting students to passively and almost vicariously absorb morality by being given good moral exemplars to follow, this is an active and meaningful student-centred approach.

Application of moral reasoning across the curriculum

As a means to encourage the development of moral reasoning, the study of moral dilemmas through literature, film, subject application, current affairs, personal experience or relationships, and the teaching of moral reasoning strategies in this context, has valuable applications. Subjects studied not simply for their technical worth, but also for the understanding of social conditions and contexts that they can engender in students, will 'feed their moral interest and develop moral insight' (Dewey in Rice, 1996). Examples of possible moral dilemmas across a range of curriculum areas could include:

- advertising: Should young viewers be the targets of advertising?
- arts: Should artistic works be subject to censorship?
- business studies: Should commodities always be built to last?
- current affairs: Should children of asylum seekers be educated in regular schools while in detention?

- film studies: Should students under sixteen study films with an M15+ (Mature adult) rating?
- legal studies: Should repeat speeding offenders be put into prisons?
- mathematics: Are statistics the basis for misinformation?
- philosophy: Is stealing always wrong?
- physical education: Should athletes take performance-enhancing drugs?
- religious studies: Should Australian schools teach children about Christian religious festivals?
- science: Is space exploration worth the money and the risk?
- society and environment: Should governments work against globalisation?

Not only can moral reasoning be applied across the curriculum, it should be applied in all areas to maximise students' efficacy. Teachers should not assume that reasoning strategies are automatically transferred to contexts in which they are not explicitly taught.

Discussing concepts

Just as there are common principles underpinning moral reasoning, there are also overarching concepts that can be explored through the material being discussed in the selected moral dilemma. Concepts are pivotal in our lives. They help us understand ourselves, the way our world works and how we connect to it. Concepts such as love, friendship, culture and responsibility are difficult to precisely define to the satisfaction of all people, but they are nonetheless universally relevant. Exploring 'big picture' concepts adds meaning and wonder to our intellectual pursuits. Concepts such as freedom could be explored through the stories of the Stolen Generations in a study of Australian history. The concept of beauty could be explored through a health and physical education discussion about anorexia. Looking for patterns and connections is another overarching concept that adds greater depth and enrichment to the experience.

The importance of effective questioning

Good questions fuel good thinking and are an important skill to master. The teacher's role in developing students' moral reasoning skills is that of a facilitator. They can, for example, ask relevant questions that focus or move the discussion along. The teacher should deflect questions back to the students, and avoid dominating the discussion. The aim is to encourage students to think for themselves and to generate their own questions, while avoiding endless examples and personal stories. Some classes may need to spend time specifically looking at the different types and purposes of questions in the context of critical thinking skills. As a general rule, questions should be clear, key and inclusive.

Because moral reasoning involves both critical and caring thinking skills, some question starters based on Bloom's Taxonomy of Cognitive Objectives and Krathwohl's Taxonomy of Affective Objectives have been suggested in the following tables. Teachers can use these to form discussion questions or assignment topics. Through the process of reasoning, stimulated by good questioning, students will gain a knowledge and understanding of the issue, and be able to analyse and evaluate all the relevant facts and opinions. They can then construct or hypothesise solutions or new ways to view the problem.

PAVE Moral Reasoning Strategy

Thoughtful question starters

Bloom's Taxonomy of Cognitive Objectives	
Levels of Taxonomy	To encourage good critical thinking: Question starters
Remembering This is the information level, which asks for the facts and definitions, and clarifies the purpose of the discussion. It seeks to determine the evidence underlying what we think, and to ascertain what we know.	What are the facts? Who is involved? What is the problem? What happened? Where and when did it happen? What proof is there … ? Please remind me of the facts about … ?
Understanding This is the interpretation level of questioning, which seeks explanations and illustrations of the facts and helps to clarify understanding.	What do you find puzzling? What do you mean by … ? Why is this a problem? For whom is it a problem? Why do you say that? How does that relate to what … said? Can you say that in another way? I'm no expert, so perhaps you could explain that to me? Can you repeat what … just said in your own words? Have you made any assumptions when you say … ? Can you give an example of … ? Can you explain why … acted that way/said that? Can we clarify that point? What could have happened if … ? Can you expand upon what you just said?
Applying Once students understand the facts and issues, they can apply this knowledge in meaningful ways. If responses indicate flaws in their understanding or interpretation of the facts, the teacher may need to summarise and display what the class knows on the board, or task the class to write down their own summaries of relevant facts.	Do you know of a similar problem? How was that solved? Could that resolution apply here? Can you think of a situation where (this suggestion/idea etc) would not work? What questions would you ask a particular person involved if you could? Can you list of all the pros and cons of that idea? Could you report the main ideas in a newsflash?

Levels of Taxonomy:	To encourage good critical thinking: Question Starters
Analysing Being able to break down the 'big picture' into its component parts can help students distinguish the faults and strengths in arguments. It also helps identify what is or isn't relevant, and any assumptions or generalisations that undermine moral reasoning.	Is that a good enough reason? If that is true, what else is true? If that is true, what then must be false? What consequences will follow? Who is most positively/negatively affected by this? What motivation was there to do this? At what point did things change? What problems did that cause? What positive outcomes happened as a result? Is that an assumption?
Evaluating Holding up ideas to check and judge their worth or appropriateness to the task is an important executive thinking skill. It is important that students can give reasons for their judgements.	Are our sources reliable? Is this point relevant? How do we know … ? Do you agree with … ? What is one solution? How can you justify that? What would you say if you were the judge/prosecutor? What reasons did you find most convincing? Is there a better solution? Are these two ideas compatible/different/the same? Does that person simply act/react, or do they consider?
Creating These questions ask students to look at creative solutions, or to look beyond the situation. Creative questions can be asked at any time and, in the spirit of the Community of Inquiry, all contributions are accepted. Lateral and creative thinking is valued.	How else could that be interpreted/viewed? What would you change if you could? What questions could we ask to move forward? How could you best do that? What decisions have we made? What implications can be drawn? Where do we go from here? What could you propose?

© 2011 Hawker Brownlow Education • 9781742392547 • HB2547

Krathwohl's Taxonomy of Affective Objectives	
Levels of Taxonomy	To encourage good caring thinking: Question Starters
Receiving This is the level of thinking where the student displays awareness, listens, notices and observes. Information is received through all senses.	What do you notice about this? What did you hear … say? How did that make you feel? How would you feel if … ?
Responding Students are encouraged to discuss or explain their thoughts and ideas. In sharing with others, students are often able to crystallise and clarify their own thoughts while receiving valuable feedback.	Can you suggest why that might be? Can you offer a way to proceed from here? What was your initial reaction? How do you feel about it now? What should we think about first?
Valuing The student chooses a concept, position or behaviour that they believe is worthy. It is not a matter of being told what is important, but what the student values.	How could you defend … ? What would you like to see happen here? What appeals to you most about … ? Whose idea do you identify with most closely? What do you disagree with?
Organising The student reviews, questions and arranges values and ideas into an ordered system or plan.	Which of your values can be applied here to give some structure? How can you figure out … ? What is the best choice, based on what you care about?
Characterising When asking students to connect with a problem in an emotional way, they need to have some positive outcome or resolution as an outlet for their feelings. 'Characterising' asks a student to live their beliefs. The student voices their beliefs and affirms their values.	What can you say to affirm each position? Which person involved is someone in whom you would confide? If you believed someone's actions to be wrong, what would you do? Do you respect someone who changes their mind? How would you have behaved?

Applying the PAVE moral reasoning strategy

Principles. Agreements. Virtues. End consequences.

The moral reasoning strategy outlined in this chapter borrows heavily from other problem-solving strategies, particularly Maker's (1995) discussion of moral dilemmas based on Kohlberg's (1964) theory of moral development, and Ruggiero's (1997) analysis of ethical issues. By including a consideration of the major philosophical schools of thought, this strategy gives the moral reasoner additional knowledge and skills with which to deliberate at greater depth and understanding. When discussing moral dilemmas, one assumption made is that people generally seek to do the right thing. The central questions are:

- What could I do that is morally right?
- What should I do in this situation?
- What will I do?
- Why will I choose that course of action?

Rather than allowing students to act and react without thinking, the moral reasoning strategy advocated encourages them to reflect on these very important questions. The strategy empowers them to make reasoned moral choices, to understand the basis of others' moral choices, and to develop skills with which to negotiate positive outcomes. The strategy is outlined on a Resource Sheet on page 36.

PAVE Moral Reasoning Strategy

1. Define the moral dilemma.
2. Establish the context.
3. Consider multiple moral perspectives:
   - Principles
   - Agreements
   - Virtues
   - End consequences
4. Evaluation of alternatives.
5. Individual choice of action.
6. Community of Inquiry discussion, in pairs or small groups.
7. Whole class discussion.
8. Individual reflection.

Stepping through the PAVE strategy: A teaching plan

In the ensuing text is a specific example of a moral dilemma entitled 'The exam dilemma'. What follows is an explanation of specific tasks to be undertaken at each step of the PAVE moral reasoning strategy, and some suggestions about the ways in which the teacher can facilitate the process. After each step, we return to how this could apply to choosing the right thing to do in 'The exam dilemma', by way of illustration.

The exam dilemma

Imagine yourself in the following situation:

Your friend, Greg, has somehow managed to obtain answers to the examination you are both about to take. He offers them to you and to another friend of his, Jane, and swears you both to secrecy. A high mark in the exam will make your parents very happy. They've spent tens of thousands of dollars they could barely afford on your school fees, to give you the best educational opportunities.

What would you do?

Step 1: Define the moral dilemma and identify who is affected by it

Having perceived that a moral dilemma exists, the first step is to restate the dilemma. What exactly is the moral question involved? Integral to identifying the dilemma is the identification of all those involved. Who will be affected by the outcome? Students who are morally sensitive will quickly identify a moral issue. In order to discuss the dilemma, all students need to understand the issues involved and to be able to identify who will be affected. In the classroom, this step can be taken as a group, to ensure that all students are clear about the nature of the problem.

Defining the exam dilemma

- What is the dilemma?

- Should I cheat to make sure I do well in the examination?

- Do I keep quiet, or tell the teacher what Greg has told me?

- Although I am the central focus, my choice will impact on others, including my parents, my teacher, my school and my friends. This is illustrated in the following relationship chart.

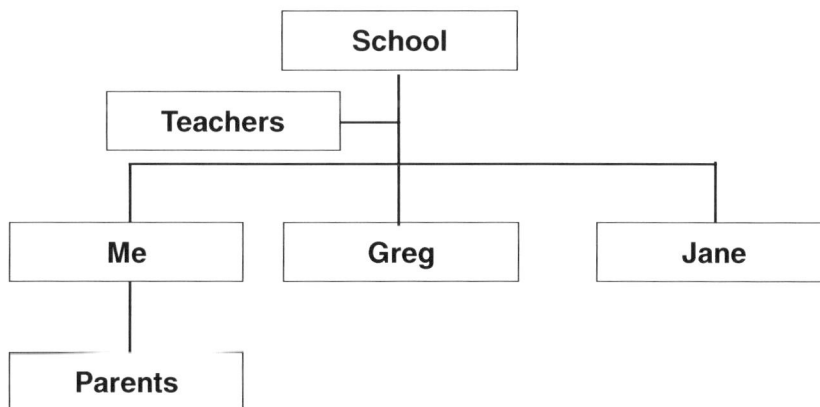

```
                    School
        Teachers ────┤
        ┌────────────┼────────────┐
       Me          Greg          Jane
        │
     Parents
```

Step 2: Establish the context

- Students need to be clear about all the relevant facts. It is important to establish where and when the situation occurs, as context is critical in deciding upon the right action.

- Perhaps not all of the details necessary for making a decision are obvious, and questions may need to be asked to clarify the context of the dilemma.

- If not all of the necessary information is available, then some speculations and assumptions may need to be made in order to advance.

- Younger children should be given as much information as they need. They could identify the questions needing answers, and the teacher could then provide the necessary information. Alternatively, the teacher could give all required information at the outset.

- Older children should be encouraged to ask 'what if' questions, and to entertain a complexity of possibilities.

Again, the PAVE reasoning strategy depends upon these two initial steps being taken as a group, to ensure that each student has the knowledge they need to make a reasonable choice.

The context of the exam dilemma

What is known and what questions remain about the situation?

Known:

- I am about to sit for my exam.
- I need to get good marks to guarantee I pass the year.
- My parents are not wealthy.
- My parents have spent a large sum of money on my education.
- Greg is my friend.
- Greg has obtained the answers for the exam.
- Greg has offered to give the answers to me and to his friend Jane.

Unknown:

- How did Greg get the answers?
- Does anyone else know about it?
- What if other people have found the answers, just like Greg?
- How safe will it be to use the answers? Can we be found out?
- Is Greg's friend, Jane, trustworthy?
- Are the answers genuine?
- How long is it before the exam?
- Do my parents have high expectations of me, or am I putting pressure on myself to do well?
- How confident am I of being able to do well on my own merits?

Step 3: Consider four ethical perspectives

The next step is a detailed process involving the scrutiny of facts in relation to each of the four ways of thinking about ethics: principles, agreements, virtues and end consequences. Refer to Chapter One for a closer examination of each of these four perspectives. The Resource Sheet on page 11, which summarises the key ideas of each of the four perspectives, is a useful resource that could be displayed to remind students about the main focus of each school of thought. Each of these perspectives offers a particular criteria to help solve the moral dilemma of 'what ought to be done' by imposing ethical imperatives and a sense of order. Considered in isolation, however, each ethical perspective has limitations. Looking at the dilemma from all four perspectives is like examining a botanical specimen using four different procedures. Each procedure will reveal the specimen in a different light and help to ascertain its nature, but a more complete understanding is possible by referring to all four forms of analysis. During this process, students should be given guidance to help them understand the criteria and limitations of each perspective, and about how each perspective would help determine the right action in this particular situation. Question prompts for each of the ethical perspectives are included as Resource Sheets. These are designed to help students work through a detailed consideration of the dilemma using a particular ethical focus.

- Although these sheets are intended as student worksheets, the teacher could initially guide the students through this step and work through the sheets as a class.

- Each student could be asked to examine the dilemma from each of the four perspectives.

- The class could be divided into four groups, with each group tasked to explore the dilemma from one ethical perspective only. Following these discussions, the class could be brought back together to share their findings.

- The class could be divided into groups of four students and, using a 'jigsaw' approach, each student could be asked to identify the major points from one ethical perspective. Students would then report back to the group, so that each group constructs a complete picture of the dilemma as examined through the four ethical perspectives.

Scope exists to broaden students' knowledge and understanding of moral philosophy, with extension work involving an exploration of this field and further study about some of its greatest philosophers. It is hoped that students will develop their knowledge about ethics, as well as developing the necessary skills to enable them to apply this knowledge. When they have been guided through the four perspectives, students can be tasked to apply the criteria independently.

Four ethical perspectives of the exam dilemma

Principles

- If the principles of honesty and fair play apply, then stealing is wrong. Therefore, Greg should not have 'stolen' the answers. Cheating is wrong, so I would not accept Greg's offer to give me the answers, and neither Greg nor Jane should cheat either. It is not right that some people cheat and have an unfair advantage, so I should report Greg.

- But … if loyalty to one's friends is a guiding principle, then I shouldn't report Greg. Perhaps I should tell the teacher that someone has found out the answers, and the teacher could set a new exam. But if I was asked who had the answers, I would have to lie to protect Greg, and I know that lying is wrong because of the principle of honesty.

- What if I do nothing, neither cheat nor report Greg? Am I still upholding the principles?

Agreements

- Because of my relationships with other people, I have certain obligations to them.

- I owe it to my parents to do well in my exams. I don't want to let them down, but will they be disappointed in me if I cheat?

- I value my friendship with Greg and I appreciate his offer of help. I do not feel obliged to cheat just because of our friendship, but I would not feel good about betraying his secret.

- Perhaps I owe some consideration to my teacher and to my school, so I don't want to tarnish their reputation by cheating. But have they fulfilled their obligation to me and properly prepared me for this exam? If I don't feel supported by them, should I feel obliged to worry about them?

- Since Jane is Greg's friend, I feel no sense of obligation to her.

Virtues

- A virtuous person is a person of good character and conscience.
- If I am virtuous, I will not cheat because I value honesty and integrity.
- I would probably try to convince Greg to not use the answers, or to confess and apologise.
- A virtuous person would value loyalty, so I probably would not report Greg. I might, however, choose to end our friendship since I would not want to be friends with someone who is dishonest.
- But ... am I a person who wants to be virtuous?

End consequences

- The best end consequences would rely on factors outside of my control, and would hinge on whether or not we were found out. Perhaps I would cheat if I was sure I could get away with it? But ... am I prepared to take risks?
- Trying to imagine all possible endpoints or consequences of my choices is difficult, as there are many unknowns to consider. Some of these are shown below:
- Can I ever truly predict all the end consequences of my choices?
- A good outcome for me might bring about unhappy outcomes for others. Whose happiness is most important?

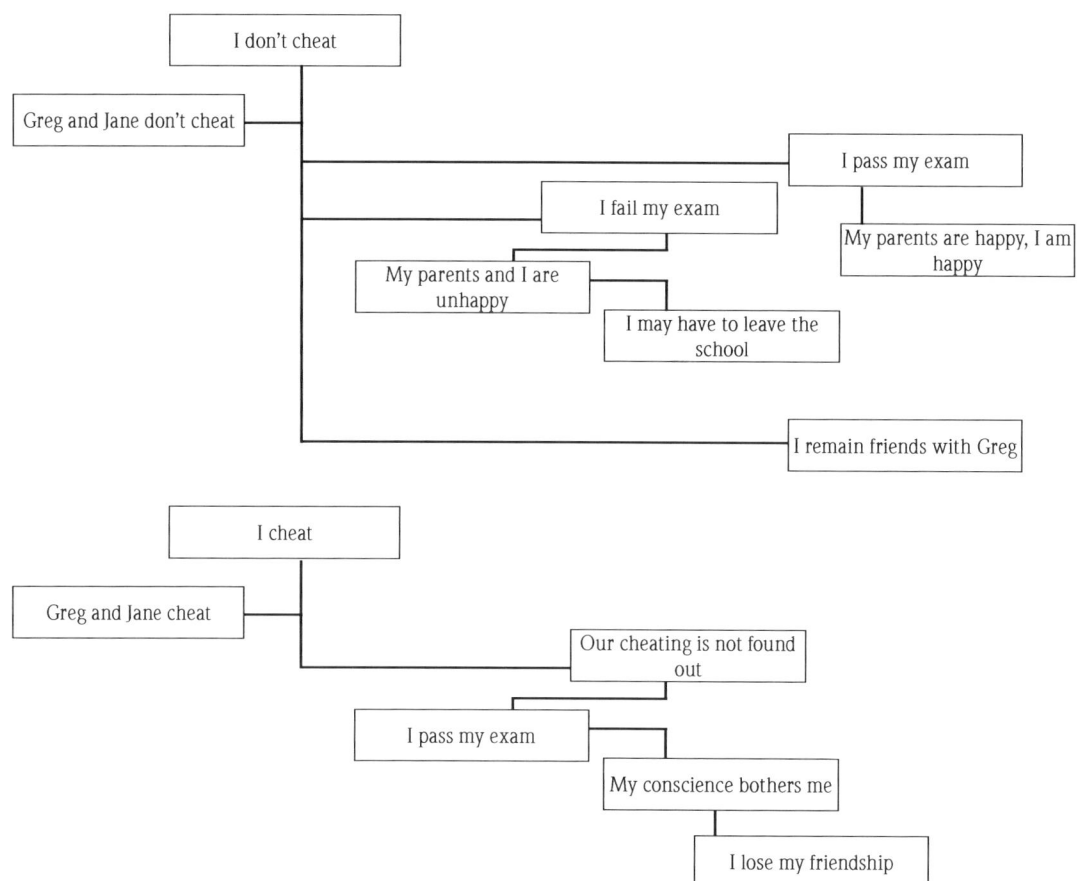

© 2011 Hawker Brownlow Education • 9781742392547 • HB2547

Step 4: Explorations of alternatives

At this point, students should be able to explain what each person or interest group would want to happen, and why. This is especially important because students may identify with only one of the people involved, but a well-reasoned choice will consider all points of view. Students need to empathise with others in order to understand that different people may have needs and priorities that differ from their own. Role-play can be a useful way to enable students to 'try on' different attitudes and perspectives.

Evaluating the alternatives of the exam dilemma

- My parents want me to do well. I hope that they would support me if I honestly did the best I could do, even if it meant repeating the year.

- Greg doesn't care if I cheat or not. He does not want to be found out, so he trusts me not to report him. He would be very unhappy if I reported him.

- The school is a fee-paying institution, likely based on Christian values. Their students are their best advertisement, so they want them to succeed academically and demonstrate good character.

- I want to do well. If I am confident of doing well on my own, I will not cheat. If I am not confident I might cheat, but will my conscience bother me? What is most important to me? Am I prepared to risk being found out? What is the worth of something obtained by dishonest means? What is the worth of a friendship with a dishonest person?

Step 5: Individual choice of action

- Having all possible courses of action and justifications at hand, the student then has to decide the overriding priority, and which criteria for judgement best 'solves' the dilemma. There will be some dilemmas where a couple of perspectives seem to carry equal importance, yet lead to different conclusions. Students may be overwhelmed by the difficulty of singling out and justifying one course of action. The teacher may need to give them guidance towards finding some way to resolve such an impasse.

- By this stage of the process, each student should be able to articulate and explain their own position about the right course of action. They still may not be completely decided, but they need to take at least a tentative position. Attaining this step may be the desired endpoint of a lesson, perhaps with the completion of Step 5 being set as a homework task. This then allows a full lesson when resuming the strategy, to discuss at length the moral choices involved.

Making an individual choice about the exam dilemma

There are many alternative justifications possible. Will I cheat? Will I report Greg? These are my two choices, but I have to understand my underlying reasoning. Despite knowing that good results would make my parents happy, and considering the importance of my friendship with Greg, I might decide to adhere to my own sense of integrity, and fair play, and not cheat. I might also choose not to report Greg.

Step 6: Community of Inquiry discussion

When we decide on a course of action, we need to be able to communicate our decision to others, and to be able to offer reasons that support our decision, in the context of the Community of Inquiry (see Chapter Two).

- This step requires students to share their ideas in pairs, small groups and, finally, as a whole class. The pairs and groups could be composed of students who agree on a course of action, and at this point they can share their reasons for their decision. This should help students to clarify and consolidate their own positions, as well as listening to and considering others' points of view. Each student needs to be able to present their choice of action, and to defend it with clear justifications.

- The conduct and the code of the Community of Inquiry, explained in Chapter Two, are assumed to be known and practised throughout these discussions.

- Time is always a critical factor in this step. The lesson may end before the group has collectively arrived at a satisfactory point of agreement. If this is the case, some students may feel frustrated because they still have no 'answer' to the dilemma. Although philosophers love endless discussions, students tend to be less patient. The process of discussion is almost as important as reaching consensus. However, it is important to give each discussion some closure. Before the lesson ends, take some time to summarise the discussion so far, to note the progress the group has made and to identify the different positions taken, possibly even to ask the students to signal which position they agree with by a show of hands. Alternatively, students could stand on a number line to indicate how satisfied they felt at the end of the discussion, from 0 (not at all) to 10 (very satisfied).

Step 7: Individual reflection

- It may be that the student's original position about the right thing to do has been reinforced as a consequence of the Community of Inquiry discussion.

- It may be that the student's choice remains unaltered, but that the reasons for holding this view have changed.

- Perhaps the group discussion has caused the student to rethink their original choice.

Ultimately, students need to make autonomous decisions, and they should be able to communicate the reasons behind their choices. Whatever the outcome, thinking about thinking, or metacognition, is a conscious, self-evaluative process that consolidates the reasoning process and helps reconcile any concerns. This step may be completed as a homework task, or it may be possible to allow lesson time during which students are able to reflect, while their focus is maintained.

Some students may need guidance to channel their reflections in a more constructive form. Pro forma sheets can be devised that ask students to answer specific questions about their choices, or to choose the most helpful comment that was made or the most difficult aspect of the dilemma. Existing strategies, such as de Bono's Six Hats and PMI, could be also applied. Caring thinking strategies that ask students to express how they felt, what they valued, what the ideal outcome for them would be and what they could do to make it happen, can also be helpful. Examples of these ideas are included as a Resource Sheet at the end of this chapter.

What else needs to be considered?

Ethical reasoning attempts to synthesise different views that are, in a sense, rival views. Although the aim is to achieve a decision that is good or right, the process is as significant as the outcome. The reasoning process is an interplay between its parts, which are connected by their conflict into a dynamic tension of logic and debate. Metacognition, or reflection, is the key to achieving a personal commitment to an outcome.

When analysing ethical dilemmas, there are some inherent dangers. Some students may see issues clearly framed by rigid and inflexible rules. Such an absolutist position needs to be avoided, and careful navigation through the discussion may be required, to encourage open-mindedness without criticism of personal values. The opposite position, where a student gives credence to all possible courses of action as equally deserving and a matter of personal preference, is also undesirable. This leads to relativism, where 'anything goes', which is clearly not a reasonable position to uphold. Other dangers to be aware of include making generalisations, unwarranted assumptions or over-simplifications, applying double standards and reaching hasty conclusions. The mentoring role of the teacher is essential in monitoring the discussion, controlling the quality of the exchange and encouraging the development of positive critical thinking habits.

Will good ethical reasoning ensure good ethical action?

Human beings may choose to act ethically, or they may choose otherwise. Rational, independent thinkers make decisions after considering all the information at hand, and reflecting upon their knowledge base and making connections between their knowledge and understanding. They support their decisions with sound reasoning. Whether or not a person chooses to act ethically in all situations is dependent not necessarily on their capacity for ethical reasoning, but on other personality factors that provide the motivation for ethical behaviour. An ethically developed person is one who cares about ethical issues, understands ethical issues and acts ethically when dealing with other people (Jewell, 2000).

A distinction must be drawn between advanced ethical reasoning and advanced ethical development. The former implies the abstract intellectual ability to recognise an ethical issue and decide upon the 'right' outcome. The latter implies the practical application of the ethical imperative. This requires other personality factors, such as courage, autonomy and altruism. The best ethical choices will be made by those who are able to reason well, and who also desire to do the right thing.

Conclusion

Children of every age need social skills, for life is communal and building social relationships is integral to it. As youngsters, they are taught to follow rules. As children develop, they start to see themselves as individuals, and questions of identity and the nature of relationships arise. They start to question the rules. For adolescents emerging from a childhood of relative certainties into an adult world of rights, responsibilities and often-conflicting pressures, choosing the right thing to do can be one of their most difficult challenges. In all aspects of adult life, individuals are called upon to make decisions and choices that will impact either positively or negatively upon their own and others' happiness and well-being.

By guiding students through the process of ethical reasoning, teachers can help them to make the transition from an orientation towards personal interests to an appreciation of social responsibility, thus facilitating their moral development. Ethical reasoning strategies can be taught, enabling students to become more skilled at evaluating and justifying ethical choices. Whether the development of ethical reasoning can generate an increased capacity for higher moral development, is a question to be explored more fully in another context.

The strong imperative for teachers is to assist students to make good choices, to want to make good choices and to teach with this aim in mind. This essential element of life preparation is often left to chance, and not given specific guidance. A moral climate can be established in the classroom where reasoning skills can be taught, knowledge of the nature of ethics can be imparted, and practice can be given to encourage the development of cognitive and affective skills and dispositions conducive to making good ethical choices. Part of our task as teachers is to impart the 'wisdom of the elders' to the students in our care, and to inspire the belief that the ethical life is a worthwhile pursuit. This will empower students with the knowledge, skills and dispositions to make well-informed and reasoned moral choices. Then two important consequences should follow: Firstly, each student's individual development will be enhanced and, secondly, the moral fibre of society will be strengthened (Jewell 2005).

PAVE moral reasoning strategy

1. Define the moral dilemma.

2. Establish the context.

3. Consider multiple moral perspectives:
   - Principles
   - Agreements
   - Virtues
   - End consequences.

4. Evaluation of alternatives.

5. Individual choice of action.

6. Community of Inquiry discussion:
   - pairs
   - small groups
   - whole class.

7. Individual reflection.

© 2011 Hawker Brownlow Education • 9781742392547 • HB2547

PAVE moral reasoning strategy: Principles

According to people who favour principles, what makes an action right is whether it adheres to principles, or moral rules that apply to any set of circumstances. Principles are not the same as laws, although many laws are based on principles, such as: children need protection, always tell the truth, be fair, etc.

In any moral dilemma being discussed there are several possible courses of action, each of which can be justified in some way. Your task is to examine each of these choices by discovering and considering the underlying principles involved. The right course of action will best honour the principles at stake.

1. Identify the principle/s relevant to this dilemma.

2. List all the possible courses of action.

3. Consider the following questions in the light of the principles and alternative choices of action possible in solving this moral dilemma:

   - Are there people involved who value different principles?

   - Are some principles more important than others?

   - How do you decide?

   - Why would a person ever choose to do something that they know to be wrong?

4. After considering all the alternative choices, decide which action is the most principled choice.

5. Does this perspective enable you to satisfactorily choose the right action?

6. What other questions arose as you thought about the principles involved?

Looking deeper

- Are there any principles here that would hold true in all situations?

- Is the only appropriate motive for moral action to obey a set of principles?

- Describe a person from real life or literature who you think is 'a person of principle'. Explain why you would/would not like to be friends with them.

PAVE moral reasoning strategy: Agreements

According to people who favour using agreements, what makes an action right is whether it is consistent with what the people involved agree should happen. People willingly enter into contracts with each other, either formally or informally, written or spoken, about the way they agree to treat each other. As a result, they have expectations of each other.

In the moral dilemma being discussed, there are several possible courses of action, each of which can be justified in some way. Your task is to examine each of these choices by considering what social contracts or agreements are in place, and what the expectations and obligations are of the people involved.

1. Identify the relationships between each of the individuals or groups involved, and determine if there are any existing agreements between them. A good way to represent this is by drawing a concept map.

2. List all the possible courses of action.

3. For each choice of action, consider the following questions:

   - Are all of the people or groups involved aware that there is an agreement in place?
   - Are there any agreements which have conflicting responsibilities?
   - How would you decide if some agreements are more important than others?
   - Is there a way to resolve this dilemma without breaking any social agreements?

4. After considering all the alternative choices, decide which action respects the agreements in place.

5. Does this perspective enable you to satisfactorily choose the right action?

6. What other questions arose as you worked through the agreements?

Looking deeper

- Is loyalty to your group of friends always right?
- Should people be able to please themselves about what they do, without considering others?
- How do we treat people with whom we have no agreements?

PAVE moral reasoning strategy: Virtues

According to people who favour virtues, what makes an action right is whether it is what a virtuous person would do. Virtues are character traits, like courage, compassion and integrity. A virtuous person will always do the right thing out of habit, because it is in their character to do so.

In the moral dilemma being discussed, there are several possible courses of action, each of which can be justified in some way. Your task is to examine each of these choices by asking, 'What is the virtuous thing to do?'

1. List all the possible courses of action.

2. For each choice of action, consider the following questions:

   • What sort of person would choose to behave in this way?

   • If actions speak louder than words, then what do the actions of the people involved reveal about their characters?

   • What character traits do you think are most virtuous?

   • If people do not have these character traits, does that make them bad people?

3. After considering all the alternative choices, decide which action a virtuous person would choose.

4. Does this perspective enable you to satisfactorily choose the right action?

5. What other questions arose as you worked through the virtues?

Looking deeper

• If no one is there to witness our actions, does it matter if we don't do the right thing?

• Choose an outstanding person, such as Mandela, Gandhi or someone that you know (yourself perhaps?), and examine their life. Would you say that this person acted virtuously? Why?

• Examine an ordinary person, or even yourself, and compare their virtues with the outstanding person's. What similarities or differences in virtues are there between them?

PAVE moral reasoning strategy: End consequences

According to people who look at the end consequences, what makes an action right is whether the end consequences which follow as a result of it are good. That is, whether the action increases the welfare of the people affected by it. By 'good', we might mean happiness, well-being, pleasure, interest or satisfaction.

In the moral dilemma being discussed, there are several possible courses of action, each of which can be justified in some way. Your task is to examine each of these choices by considering what the end consequences of each choice would be, in order to select the right action. That is, the action which produces the best outcome.

1. List all the possible courses of action.

2. For each choice of action, consider the following questions:

   - What are the consequences of the action for the main person involved? Short term/long term? Good/bad?
   - What are the consequences for the other people involved?
   - Short term/long term? Good/bad?
   - Would this action result in positive outcomes for most of the people involved?
   - Whose welfare or happiness is most important?

3. After considering all of the alternative choices, decide which action results in the best outcome for the most people.

4. Does this perspective enable you to satisfactorily choose the right action?

5. What other questions arose as you worked through the consequences?

Looking deeper

- Can you think of an action that may be right in one set of circumstances, but wrong in a different situation, because of the consequences of that action?
- Can you always foresee all the consequences resulting from your actions?
- Do you proceed even though the action may make fewer people happy?

© 2011 Hawker Brownlow Education • 9781742392547 • HB2547

PAVE moral reasoning strategy: Reflection

In the moral dilemma being discussed, there are several possible courses of action, each of which can be justified in some way. Your task is to examine each of these choices in the light of the four moral perspectives, to engage in discussion and ultimately to decide upon the right thing to do. You must be able to explain the reasons behind your choice.

Possible ways to reflect on the PAVE process

Consider the following questions:

1. Did you fully understand the nature of the dilemma at the outset?

2. As you progressed, did the problem seem to become clearer or more complex?

3. Did you have all the necessary facts to enable you to make the right decision?

4. Were you able to explain your reasoning in a way that others understood?

5. What questions do you have now?

6. How would you attempt to find the answers?

7. Have any of your ideas changed through this process?

8. How useful do you think this strategy would be if you applied it to making good moral choices in your own life?

PMI Evaluation

Plus:

- What do you think are all the positive things about the PAVE strategy you have undertaken to resolve the dilemma?

- What did you enjoy about the discussion?

- What was an interesting point made in the discussion?

- What helped you most to reach a decision?

Minus:

- What did you think was least useful about the PAVE strategy?

- What didn't you like about the discussion?

- What was an example of an unreasonable statement made?

- What was said that challenged your point of view?

Interesting:

- What is something that is neither good nor bad about the PAVE strategy, but worth considering next time?

- What questions do I have now?

- What would I like to know more about?

PAVE moral reasoning strategy: Reflection

Caring Thinking

Affective Thinking Includes attitudes and emotions around a clear understanding of right and wrong	How do I feel about the problem? How do I feel about the solution? With whom do I identify, or most like in this situation. Why? Who do I least like? Why?
Valuative Thinking Examines and clarifies what is important or valued	Whose actions do I approve of and why? Whose actions do I object to and why? Which course of action do I think is right? What reasons support my choice?
Normative Thinking Looks at what would happen in the ideal world and how the ideal situation aligns, or can align with reality	In a perfect world, how would the problem be resolved? What would I like to see happen? What needs to be overcome in order for this to happen?
Active Thinking Translates personal beliefs and values into action, and provides a positive outlet for caring thinking to empower meaningful behaviour.	What can/could I do to resolve the issue? Who could I depend upon to help me? How could I ensure that everyone involved accepted my resolution? What steps could be taken to prevent a similar problem in the future?

 © 2011 Hawker Brownlow Education • 9781742392547 • HB2547

Chapter 4
Ethical decision-making through stories: Using critical literacy analysis

To live is to be in a story, our own story touching the stories of others. Stories illuminate our dreams, our hopes, our goals and our values. The world is a mirror reflecting and refracting our collective stories into the story of humanity.

This chapter provides:

- a rationale for using literature in ethical decision-making
- an exemplar unit using a picture book, *The Deliverance of Dancing Bears*
- suggested other books containing ethical issues
- Resource Sheets:

    Issues raised by the story

    Discussion ideas for a Community of Inquiry

    Applying four ethical strategies

    Writing tasks

Please note: Chapters One and Two provide essential material about the conduct of ethical decision-making, and should be read in conjunction with this chapter. Chapter Eight provides evaluation and assessment tools.

A rationale for the use of stories in ethical decision-making

We all organise our lives in story form, even when simply recounting an everyday event. Our personal identity is developed through continually interpreting our experiences. We use stories to construct meaning and to give value to events that occur in our lives, and in the lives of others (Polkinghorne, 1988).

Stories provide a means of reflection. The way we relate the events in our life reflects our moral choices (Tappan, 1991). When we tell our own stories we interpret, rather then merely report, the things that happen to us. The stories of our culture shape this interpretation and thus our view of ourselves, of others and of the world in which we live. Our personal stories are connected to significant cultural stories and we relate our individual experience to shared cultural stories, particularly when seeking answers to life's questions. When we construct our life story, we explain our own feelings and actions, and thus our own moral stance. Our personal identity is really our personal story, shaped by our cultural context. We use our own 'story' as a reference to understand our life experiences. Thus, our developmental readiness to participate in our community parallels our ability to use stories to interpret life events (Bruner, 1986). As students mature, they are more able to reflect on their own feelings and actions, and to see them mirrored in the stories of others' lives.

The development of students through stories

From around ten years of age, children can summarise a plot and analyse cause and effect in an objective way. During middle school years, children are increasingly able to separate their subjective response to the story from the author's intentions. This signifies an understanding of their shared reality with others' inner psychological states and dispositions, rather than being embedded in their own. It enables students to be empathetic, experience others' viewpoints and to understand reciprocal obligations.

Readers need to be able to recognise the effect of characters' motives on the story outcomes before they can consider moral choices. They also need the capacity to identify the internal psychological states of characters, such as what they are feeling, wanting and planning. When students are able to describe characters' needs and motives, they are ready to examine the reasons for their own reactions to the stories. They can then make analogies with other literature, or other life experiences (Applebee, 1978). The plans and goals of characters provide the motivational ties that hold the story together (Kemper, 1984). Students vary in their developmental ability to understand that actions and consequences are connected to the characters' psychological and emotional needs.

Effective ways of presenting stories: Books containing ethical issues, folktales and picture books

Books containing ethical issues

There are a number of books written for middle school students containing ethical issues that range from the global to the particular concerns of adolescents. A list of some suggested titles is provided at the end of this chapter.

Folktales

Folktales and legends present perennial issues requiring moral choices. These stories allow scope for the clarification of the difference between decisions made using a 'principles' or 'consequences' approach (see Chapter One). Many myths explaining cultural origins contain conflict and violence. The various versions of the Australian Aboriginal Rainbow Serpent legend demonstrate this 'ends justifying the means' approach. The large snake swallows his own people and is then attacked by others in his cultural group. The story outcomes include the foundation of indigenous group boundaries, correct ritual performance and the creation of rainbow lorikeets. Violence is justified through the story resolution, which explains 'how things came to be'.

Folk heroes, such as Robin Hood, are characters whose actions involve a clash of principles. Stealing, violence and risk-taking are presented as acceptable moral choices if the outcome benefits 'deserving' people. Students may be challenged to make judgements about values such as honesty and integrity. Is stealing always unacceptable or are there exceptional circumstances?

Picture books

Although picture books may be regarded as written for young children, there are also benefits for older students. Our aim is to examine the ethical messages in stories. This examination can be more effective if the story's presentation is simple, so that the focus is on the message, rather than on sophisticated literary devices. Picture books have short, succinct texts that can be used as an introduction to issues, and provide visual support to enhance the text, allowing inference and speculation. They can also explore themes, such as:

- establishing one's identity
- family and community relationships
- coming to terms with disappointment and loss
- problems of justice and care
- peace and conflict
- interdependence in culture and environment.

Chapters One and Two provide ethical perspectives and ways of conducting inquiries concerning resolutions of these issues. Applied to novels, folktales and picture books, these activities allow the development of students' abilities to reason and empathise. Students can reflect upon their own beliefs about right and wrong through examining characters' intentions and moral choices, and they can exchange their views with others. They can speculate about how life experiences affect a person's judgements, and apply that speculation to the story's characters, themselves and others.

Although a story implies the author's intentions, we all make individual interpretations and connections. Students need skills in reasoning, empathising and imagining to identify issues and relate them to their own experiences. Through interaction with story, students can consider and make judgements about characters' actions and motives. They may then relate the story to experiences in their own lives so that they can begin to understand the influences on the decisions they make (Kazemek, 1986).

Students need to have practice in critical, creative and constructive thinking. Not only should thinking engage the logical and analytical mind, but also the imagination and the emotions. Our perception of situations greatly alters how we see problems and their alternative solutions (de Bono, 1998). Therefore, it is vital to foster the skills of 'perspective taking' in order to see a variety of points of view.

Students in the middle school years are able to make quite sophisticated responses to ethical issues. The clarification of their own and awareness of others' viewpoints assists them in formulating ideas about principles of justice and care for others (Linning, 1985). A literature approach to issues provides a distancing effect. Issues may be introduced at an objective level, so that students feel safe discussing issues that might otherwise be personally difficult to talk about.

An exemplar unit using a picture book

The Deliverance of Dancing Bears by Elizabeth Stanley (1994) Nedlands, Western Australia: Cygnet Books

This unit is designed to involve students in ethical decision-making about issues raised in a story. The particular story, *The Deliverance of Dancing Bears*, is used as an example, but the processes can be applied to many stories, picture books and folktales. The unit consists of five activities:

1. Reading *The Deliverance of Dancing Bears*

2. Discussion of the issues raised by the story

3. Community of Inquiry arising from Activity 2

4. Application of 'Four ways of thinking about ethics'

5. Writing Tasks

This unit can be closely linked to other areas in the curriculum, particularly English and society and environment. It can incorporate activities used in other chapters of this book, and should use the tools provided in Chapters One and Two. In addition, Chapter Three provides moral reasoning strategies that can be applied to stories.

Activity 1: Reading *The Deliverance of Dancing Bears*

The Deliverance of Dancing Bears is a sophisticated picture book that explores many philosophical issues. It is a contemporary fable about a dancing bear, whose dreams of freedom keep her alive despite the pain of her existence. A poor peasant liberates the bear, offering his savings for her freedom from torture. The crowd is apathetic at first, but becomes aware of the injustice when it is repeated with another smaller bear. The outcome of the story is influenced by the actions of the crowd and the attitude of the main character.

The story introduces issues including:

- concern for animal rights

- the power of just one voice for justice

- altruism, forgiveness and redemption

- concerns about animals in captivity

- shared community concerns.

The reading can be made purposeful and focused if the students are primed with the following questions:

- Who are the characters? How did their actions contribute to the story outcomes? Were the outcomes fair and reasonable?

- What makes people like each other? Is it actions, similar interests or personalities?

- Should we always be rewarded when we show kindness or help others?

- Should people always conform to agreed rules of conduct at home, school or in our community?

Activity 2: Discussion of the issues raised by the story

Student discussion may be stimulated with the following questions. A Resource Sheet, 'Issues raised by the story', is at the end of this chapter.

- In the story, do you think Yusuf wanted Haluk to consider:

  (a) the consequences of his actions?

  (b) his attitude to animals? or

  (c) his attitude to life?

- What are the main issues of the story for you?

- Yusuf bought the bears to save them. Were there other ways? What would be the consequences of other actions to save the bears?

- How many times do you think Yusuf would have continued to buy the bears? What sort of person would spend their life savings in this way?
- What did Yusuf want Haluk to feel?

  (a) remorse

  (b) empathy for the bears

  (c) that there were better ways of making a living, or

  (d) other feelings

- Think about how the crowd either hindered or helped the bears at the beginning and at the end of the story. Why didn't the crowd intervene until Yusuf bought the second bear?
- What do you think happened to the bears after the story? Could they exist in the wild?

Activity 3: Community of Inquiry

This activity should use 'four things a reasonable person knows' and the 'Code of Conduct for a Community of Inquiry' from Chapter Two. The following discussion ideas appear as a Resource Sheet at the end of this chapter.

Discussion ideas for a Community of Inquiry about *The Deliverance of Dancing Bears*

Tick a position (0 to 10) alongside each of the ideas listed, saying how likely you think it is that the statement is true. Compare responses with your classmates, and then make a list of other statements that you think would produce interesting discussion.

very unlikely very likely	
0 ... 1 ... 2 ... 3 ... 4 ... 5 ... 6 ... 7... 8 ... 9 ... 10	
	Buying back the bears was the best way to save them.
	Good deeds always bring rewards.
	Everyone deserves another chance to do the right thing.
	There is a limit to how long you can keep trying to do what is right if you get no result.
	It is okay to manipulate someone's thinking if most people are happy with the outcome.
	It is a good idea to mind your own business and avoid conflict if possible.
	It is important to keep face, even when you know you are in the wrong.

Activity 4: Application of the 'Four ways of thinking about ethics'

In Chapter One, four ethical strategies were outlined: principles, agreements, virtues and consequences. We have not suggested that any one of these strategies is more important than any other, but the thoughtful application of these strategies to the issues raised in the story will provide insights into a student's moral position, and a tool for reflection and the resolution of ethical problems. A Resource Sheet, 'Applying four ethical strategies', is at the end of Chapter One. The Resource Sheet, 'Applying ethics to *The Deliverance of Dancing Bears*', is at the end of this chapter.

Principles

Principles are like duties or rules that apply to any set of circumstances. So when we argue that it is never right to tell a lie, we are thinking about principles. Principles are very useful for dealing with large groups of people. Many laws are based on principles. Some common principles are: Always tell the truth. Keep your promises. Be fair. Respect others' rights.

Students can report their responses to the following:

- Are any of the characters motivated by principles? Which characters? What principles?
- Many people say the right to be free is an important principle. Does this principle only apply to people, or to animals as well?
- Do animals have rights? If so, what rights?
- Does the story suggest that there are absolute principles of right and wrong?
- Are there any principles you think you should always live by, no matter what the consequences?

Agreements

A good method of deciding the best way to treat people is to ask them how they want to be treated. People can then reach agreements about how to treat each other. A group of friends might agree to play sport on Saturdays, or a community might make laws.

Students can report their responses to the following:

- Did the crowd agree with Yusuf at the beginning of the story? At the end? What changed?
- Do different communities in different parts of the world have differing ideas about what is right or wrong? Examples?
- Is it important to talk to others about what is right, or should each person make up their own mind?
- What laws, if any, do you think the Australian community should have about the treatment of animals?

Virtues

Virtues are character traits. A virtuous person does the right thing out of habit. To put it the other way around, the right thing to do is what a virtuous person would do. Some commonly recognised virtues are integrity, courage and compassion.

Students can report on their responses to the following:

- Who are the good characters in the story? Why do you think so? What are their virtues?
- Who are the bad characters in the story? Why do you think so?

- Why do some people act for the benefit of others? Are they virtuous, or do they expect an eventual reward?
- What are the most important virtues? What are the worst vices?

Consequences

What makes an action right is whether it has good consequences. That is, whether it increases the welfare of the people affected by it. If large numbers of people are affected, we might try to consider the greatest good for the greatest number. By 'good', we might mean happiness, well-being, pleasure, interest or satisfaction.

Students can report their responses to the following:

- Who is affected by the actions of the characters?
- How does the plot lead to the outcomes and consequences of the story?
- Is it only the consequences to people that matter, or should we consider the consequences to animals? What about trees or the environment?
- Should we worry about the welfare of people (or animals) that we have never met?
- Should we break principles or agreements to attain good consequences?
- Should we tell a lie to avoid doing harm?

Activity 5: Writing tasks

A Resource Sheet, 'Writing tasks', is at the end of this chapter.

- Empathising with characters. What were the characters' motives? What made them angry, sad, or happy? Do you know people like the characters?

  Task: Make a mind map about a problem time. What happened? How did you feel? Who helped?

- Making judgements. Did you agree with what the characters did? What helped or hindered the characters?

  Task: Write a letter to the author suggesting a different ending.

- Identifying and evaluating situations. Analyse the consequences of the characters' actions. What other choices could have been made?

  Task: Write about an event in your life. Describe the choices you faced and your reasons for what you did.

- Evaluating/empathising with roles. Who is the most important character? Who is the most powerful? Which character would you like to be? Think about your roles in your family or community.

  Task: Write a brief autobiography, or write a brief fictional biography of yourself as you would like to be.

- Inferring/interpreting. What was the message of the story?

  Task: Write your own story that has a message.

Other books containing ethical issues

The above activities using *The Deliverance of Dancing Bears* can be applied to numerous other stories. Here are some suggestions, including notes on issues. The Magpies reviews are taken from 'The Source' by K. White and R. Turton, 2004. *www.magpies.net.au*

Lockie Leonard Human Torpedo

Tim Winton

Ringwood, Victoria: McPhee Gribble, 1990

Commonly used in English in year eight. Thirteen-year-old Lockie faces the same moral dilemmas that confront many middle school students, for example, 'dobbing' on others, the temptations of sex and drugs, the breaking of rules and responsibility for siblings. He has 'old-fashioned' values, and a sense of personal morality that is strongly influenced by his parents. He resists peer pressure. Vicki has different values. This makes for interesting examination. Discussion of principles and consequences arises easily from this novel.

The Outsiders

S. E. Hinton

London, United Kingdom: Collins, 1972

A strong novel, which has been used in year nine for many years. It follows the lives of a group of teenagers, as Ponyboy and his friends deal with issues of gang affiliations and the associated moral dilemmas often caused by reckless behaviour. For example, should one risk one's own life to save someone else from a burning building? Is it right to kill, even in self-defence? Is it right to kick against authority? How we make these sorts of decisions in our own lives easily flows from these questions, and the four ethical strategies of principles, consequences, agreements and virtues can be applied to making decisions and negotiating ethical agreements with others.

The Glass Mountain

Celeste Walters

St Lucia, Queensland: University of Queensland Press, 2003

Seventeen-year-old Nom has had a terrible life: abandoned by his mother, later witness to his father's death and, since the age of eleven, under the care of a biker gang, the Pit Vipers. When he snatches an old woman's bag and sees her fall to the ground, he deliberately rides into a tree. He survives, but the Pit Vipers insist that he rejoin them, and that he return the bag. Although it takes some time, he does find the owner of the purse. Essie, now a reluctant inhabitant of a nursing home, is severely depressed. Nom, with natural practicality and an essential good-heartedness, manages to draw her out when all the best efforts of the staff had failed. Prior to meeting Essie, Nom had glimpsed the possibility of a different life, so together the two plan an escape of sorts, drawing on their identification with characters in *The Wind in the Willows* (Review from Magpies). Themes in this book include: adolescents, escapes, euthanasia, freedom, friendship, gangs, inter-generational relationships, nursing homes, orphans and orphanages, speech and story characters.

Dear Nobody

Berlie Doherty

London, United Kingdom: Lions Tracks, 1992

Told in alternating voices from the two main characters, this story is immediate and conveys a range of emotions. Chris and Helen are in their last year of school and full of plans for university and their future. Then, the one time they have sex, Helen falls pregnant. Although at first agreeing to an abortion, Helen cannot bring herself to go through with it, and opts instead to carry on at school for as long as she can before dropping out. At the same time, she feels that she should stop seeing Chris. He doesn't agree. The narrative moves via Chris's journal type accounts and Helen's letters to her unborn child, addressed to 'Dear Nobody'. (Review from Magpies.) Themes in this book include: pregnancy, relationships, responsibility, schools and students.

Flowers for Algernon

Daniel Keyes

Oxford, United Kingdom: Heinemann, 1989

Algernon the mouse is extra-clever, thanks to an experimental brain operation so far tried only on animals. Charlie, the simpleton, eagerly volunteers as the first human subject. After frustrating delays and agonies of concentration, the effects begin to show and the reports steadily improve: 'Punctuation, is? fun!' But getting smarter brings cruel shocks, as Charlie realises that his merry 'friends' at the bakery, where he sweeps the floor, have all along been laughing at him and never with him. The IQ rise continues, taking him steadily past the human average to genius level and beyond, until he's as intellectually alone as the old, foolish Charlie ever was. Now, however, he is painfully aware of his isolation. Then, ominously, Algernon begins to deteriorate (review from *Amazon.com*). Themes in this book include: a consideration of the ethics of scientific advancement.

Walking Naked

Alyssa Brugman

Crows Nest, NSW: Allen & Unwin, 2002

In this novel Brugman depicts the structures of power, and shows how easily a powerful position can be undermined when dominance depends on others to maintain their allotted, inferior, places. The school setting and the cast of young female characters evokes a style reminiscent of satirical novels such as *Animal Farm*. As with that novel, the outcome is tragic. Pretty, indulged Megan is one of the top dogs in an exclusive group of schoolgirls. They have all sorts of ritual and rules, nothing is left to chance, and everything is structured and organised. The unravelling of Megan's life starts when she is sent out of class, something that regularly happened to her friend Candice, but not to her. 'I wasn't familiar with thrown-out-of-class protocol', she opines. This leads to detention and to the start of a relationship with Perdita, 'the Freak', a girl distant from 'the group'. A series of small events, chances overlooked, bad decisions and insights accumulate, until the tragic suicide of the climax (review from Magpies). Themes in this book include: alienation, control, friendship, girls, gangs, poetry, rejection, responsibility, schools, students and suicide.

The Enemy You Killed

Peter McFarlane

Ringwood, Victoria: Viking, 1996

War games in the bush with real guns encourage the possibility of real danger and real death. This is a disturbing novel about the violence which underlies society, especially that of the young. Themes in this book include: adolescents, arms and armour, gangs, hate, revenge, violence and non-violence.

Spare Parts

Sally Rogers-Davidson

Ringwood, Victoria: Penguin, 1999

In a future time that doesn't appear to be so very far away, people live socially pre-determined lives. But there is a way of escape for Subbies, who exist precariously on the violent streets working in dangerous factories. They can donate their bodies to rich citizens, Skywalkers, who want to extend their lives. This doesn't mean death for the Subby, but a new life as a cyborg, with their brain transplanted into a human-like machine. Kelty decides to take up that option, particularly as it may mean saving the life of her badly injured best friend. The outcome, however, is surprising. Kelty does not go on to be a freedom fighter for the Subbies and society does not change. Indeed, while the possibilities for unethical actions are acknowledged, the wonders of this new technology are celebrated. Kelty's mother, Jenet, who rejects her 'new' daughter, is depicted as small-minded. Kelty only escapes Subby life because of her health and appearance (review from Magpies). Themes in this book include: appearance, future, self-perception, social classes, survival, technology, transplantation of organs and tissues.

Amongst the Hidden

Margaret Haddix

London, United Kingdom: Red Fox Definitions, 2001

To the outside world, Luke does not exist. His parents conceal their third son from a society where the penalty for breaking the Population Law is harsh. Alone in the attic, he suddenly sees a girl's face in a window of the house opposite, a house where he knows two children already live. This novel looks at an issue similar to the One Child Policy in China, and at the rights of others to make such decisions and laws.

Refuge

Libby Gleeson

Ringwood, Victoria: Penguin, 1998

Andrew is a quiet boy with a love for fossils and their clear, seemingly uncomplicated messages. He is a contrast to his lively older sister Anna, with her short-lived enthusiasms. Andrew is particularly disturbed by Anna's fights with their parents, fights about protest and complacency. His parents had been activists once, but disapprove of Anna's current interests, claiming that they are shallow compared to those they fought for. Anna turns the tables when she asks them to hide an East Timorese refugee. Ignoring their refusal, she enlists Andrew in a complicated deception. Issues addressed in this novel include Andrew's need to be recognised as a person with opinions and skills, the complications of family relationships and human behaviour, contemporary middle-class Australian family life, generational conflict and Australia's role as a place of refuge in a troubled and dangerous world. The inclusion of a map and note imply that the author seems to choose Australia's failings in regard to the invasion of East Timor as her main subject, although readers beguiled by setting and characterisation might disagree (review from Magpies). Themes in this book include: brothers and sisters, conflict, dissent, East Timor, ethics, Newtown, NSW, parents and children, refugees and honesty.

Blackwater

Eve Bunting

London, United Kingdom: HarperCollins, 2000

Thirteen-year-old Brodie is unhappy with his cousin, Alex, even before he arrives to stay for the holidays. If Alex hadn't come, Brodie would have been off on a camping trip with his friend, John. Alex is a pain, an odd child craving attention and constantly boasting of his position in the gang that runs his home neighbourhood. At six o'clock one morning, Brodie takes Alex to the pond that abuts the tumultuous Blackwater River. There, he is horrified to find the undeclared love of his life, Pauline, sitting with Otis, an older boy from school, on the rock straddling the pond and the Blackwater. Jealousy takes over and Brodie swims out unseen and grabs Pauline's legs from below the rock. Otis grabs her top and both pull. Realising the stupidity of it, Brodie lets go and swims ashore only to find that the sudden release of Pauline has sent both her and Otis into the Blackwater. Brodie races down river to try to save them but to no avail. When he in turn is rescued, he finds Alex has doctored the truth and Brodie is touted as a hero. Brodie never seems to find the right moment to tell the truth, until a friend who has also witnessed the accident convinces him to do so (review from Magpies). Themes in this book include: accidents, death, drowning, jealousy, parents and children, and honesty.

Sadako

Eleanor Coer

Blackheath, NSW: Margaret Hamilton Books, 1995

Sadako gives students an opportunity to empathise with characters, and reflect upon their own life experiences. This story is about a girl's struggle with leukaemia after the Second World War. Themes in this book include: suffering, death and the search for meaning.

Rose Blanche

Roberto Innocenti

London, United Kingdom: Jonathan Cape, 1985

A challenging text with vivid pictures, this story relates to Nazi occupation in Europe, where the heroine dies in an effort to help prisoners in a concentration camp. Like *Sadako*, *Rose Blanche* ends with a theme of hope. Themes in this book include: suffering, hope and heroism.

First Light

Gary Crew

South Melbourne, Victoria: Lothian, 1993

This novel deals with a father and son's struggle for the recognition of each other's unique qualities. Although the son and father love each other, they have little idea about each other's needs and interests. Themes in this book include: parents and children, relationships and understanding.

The Watertower

Gary Crew

Adelaide, South Australia: Era Publications, 1994

A story of risk, challenge and saving face in a relationship between two boys. Themes in this book include: risk-taking and pride.

Issues raised by the story, *The Deliverance of Dancing Bears*

1. In the story, do you think Yusuf wanted Haluk to consider:

   (a) the consequences of his actions?

   (b) his attitude to animals?

   (c) his attitude to life?

2. What are the main issues of the story for you?

3. Yusuf bought the bears to save them. Were there other ways? What would be the consequences of other actions to save the bears?

4. How many times do you think Yusuf would have continued to buy the bears? What sort of person would spend their life savings in this way?

5. What did Yusuf want Haluk to feel?

   (a) remorse

   (b) empathy for the bears

   (c) that there were better ways of making a living

   (d) other feelings

6. Think about how the crowd either hindered or helped the bears at the beginning and at the end of the story. Why didn't the crowd intervene until Yusuf bought the second bear?

7. What do you think happened to the bears after the story finished? Could they exist in the wild?

Discussion ideas for a Community of Inquiry about *The Deliverance of Dancing Bears*

Tick a position (0 to 10) alongside each of the ideas listed, saying how likely you think it is that the statement is true. Compare responses with your classmates. Then make a list of other statements that you think would produce interesting discussion.

very unlikely very likely	
0 ... 1 ... 2 ... 3... 4 ... 5 ... 6 ... 7... 8 ... 9 ... 10	
	Buying back the bears was the best way to save them.
	Good deeds always bring rewards.
	Everyone deserves another chance to do the right thing.
	There is a limit to how long you can keep on trying to do what is right if you get no result.
	It is okay to manipulate someone's thinking if most people are happy with the outcome.
	It is a good idea to mind your own business and avoid conflict if possible.
	It is important to keep face, even when you know you are in the wrong.

Applying ethics to *The Deliverance of Dancing Bears*

(To be used with the Resource Sheet, 'Four ways of thinking about ethics')

Principles

Are any of the characters motivated by principles? Which characters? What principles?

Many people say that the right to be free is an important principle. Does this principle only apply to people, or to animals as well?

Do animals have rights? If so, what rights?

Does the story suggest that there are absolute principles of right and wrong?

Are there any principles you think you should always live by, no matter what the consequences?

Agreements

Did the crowd agree with Yusuf at the beginning of the story? At the end? What changed?

Do different communities in different parts of the world have differing ideas on what is right or wrong? Examples?

Is it important to talk to others about what is right, or should each person make up their own mind?

What laws, if any, do you think the Australian community should have about the treatment of animals?

Virtues

Who are the good characters in the story? Why do you think so? What are their virtues?

Who are the bad characters in the story? Why do you think so?

Why do some people act for the benefit of others? Are they virtuous, or do they expect an eventual reward?

What are the most important virtues? What are the worst vices?

Consequences

Who is affected by the actions of the characters?

How does the plot lead to the outcomes and consequences of the story?

Is it only the consequences to people that matter, or should we consider the consequences to animals? What about trees or the environment?

Should we worry about the welfare of people (or animals) that we have never met?

Should we break principles or agreements to get good consequences? Should we tell a lie to avoid doing harm?

Writing tasks

Empathising with characters

1. What were the characters' motives? What made them angry, sad or happy? Do you know people like these characters?

   Task: Make a mind map about a problem time. What happened? How did you feel? Who helped?

2. Making judgements

   Did you agree with what the characters did? What helped or hindered the characters?

   Task: Write a letter to the author suggesting a different ending.

3. Identifying and evaluating situations

   Analyse the consequences of the characters' actions. What other choices could have been made?

   Task: Write about an event in your life, your choices and your reasons.

4. Evaluating/Empathising with roles

   Who is the most important character? Who is the most powerful? What character would you like to be? Think about your roles in your family or community.

   Task: Write a brief autobiography, or write a brief fictional biography of yourself as you would like to be.

5. Inferring/interpreting

   What was the message of the story?

   Task: Write your own story that has a message.

 © 2011 Hawker Brownlow Education • 9781742392547 • HB2547

Chapter 5
Using statistics in ethical decision-making

Please note: Chapters One and Two provide essential material about the conduct of ethical decision-making, and should be read in conjunction with this chapter. Chapter Eight provides evaluation and assessment tools.

A rationale for integrating statistics and ethics

Social and political issues involve ethical decisions which affect large numbers of people. They also involve a number of claims that invite critical thinking. Consider, for example, the question of whether immigration takes jobs away from Australians. In the following conversation there is disagreement about immigration policy.

'Our population is too high. The environment can't handle it. We need to do something to reduce the population.'

'How about lowering the immigration rate?'

'We can't do that! The whole world's overpopulated. We need to increase immigration.'

'Increasing immigration will take jobs away from Australians.'

'No it won't, immigration supports economic growth.'

'And we don't want our population to get too low. That'll really wreck the economy.'

One of the ways students can decide whether a statement is true is to make observations. A particular student might know someone who is unemployed, and they might know a recent immigrant who is employed. They might therefore think that immigration takes jobs away from Australians. However, such anecdotal evidence is not enough to establish the truth of that belief, although it might provide a reason for suggesting it as a possibility. A more reliable way of deciding whether the belief is true would be to make a large number of observations. From those observations, students could infer whether or not the claim is true. Voilà! Now they are practising statistics.

Making ethical decisions relies on understanding the nature of a problem and its potential solutions. This understanding often depends upon applying statistical knowledge, skills and strategies. Statistics are all around us. They can help us to understand a situation, usually from a 'big picture' perspective, and they are used as evidence to justify arguments or decisions.

When people become interested in a public issue, they often do so without any idea of what relevant statistics might reveal. The less the general public knows about how to accurately interpret statistical data and information, and about what questions should be asked about it, the more it is vulnerable to manipulation by parties with vested interests. Statistics can easily be misinterpreted or presented in a misleading way. Students need to learn to gather, present and interpret statistical information accurately, and to recognise misleading statistics. Since government decisions about ethical issues are responsive to community pressure, it is vitally important that people are adequately prepared with the ability to use statistical knowledge, skills and strategies in the service of ethical decision-making.

Like ethics, statistics has applications across the curriculum. Also, like ethics, statistics involves problem solving, reasoning and proof. Combining statistics and ethics enables students to better consolidate these skills more effectively than studying either discipline on its own.

Australian population and resources: An ethics and statistics unit

This unit is designed to involve students in statistical problem solving, and research, in the pursuit of ethical decision-making. It is aimed at middle school students and could be used in a number of different contexts. It consists of seven coordinated learning activities:

Activity 1: Brainstorm

Activity 2: Community of Inquiry

Activity 3: Facts versus values

Activity 4: Misleading statistics

Activity 5: Survey: Using statistics to consider consequences and reach agreements

Activity 6: Research project

Activity 7: Unit review and evaluation

The activities are flexible in terms of depth and time required, but four to six weeks on the unit is recommended. This unit provides a significant opportunity for cross-curricular collaboration, particularly between society and environment, Australian studies, English, philosophy and mathematics. Activities from other chapters in this book can be incorporated into the unit.

Activity 1: Brainstorm

Conduct a class brainstorm to determine what is already known or believed about the issue of Australian population and resources. During the brainstorm, it is important to suspend judgement. Brainstorming is a generative activity, not an analytical or evaluative one. Some of the statements generated in this brainstorm can then be included in the following Community of Inquiry session.

Activity 2: Community of Inquiry

Conduct a Community of Inquiry on the issue using the guidelines found in Chapter Two. Students can be supplied with photocopies of the Resource Sheet at the end of this chapter, entitled 'Discussion ideas for a Community of Inquiry on Australian population and resources'. This discussion naturally leads into the research phase at the core of this unit, since it will not take long for the question, 'How do we know?', to emerge. It is common for people to form opinions quickly on the basis of their own assumptions, or the opinions of others. Statistical research provides an opportunity to develop an evidence-based approach to ethical decision-making. If, for example, we focus on the question, 'Should we raise the level of immigration to Australia?', an interesting range of further questions is likely to emerge, such as:

- What is the current population? How has this changed over time?
- What size population should Australia have?
- What is the current immigration rate?
- What effect does the rate of immigration have on population?
- What are our environmental obligations?
- What effect does immigration have on Australian society?
- What are our obligations to people already living in Australia?
- What are the current migration trends?
- What factors influence migration trends?
- What are our obligations to people living in other countries?
- Is the rate of immigration all that matters?
- What type of migrants should we allow?

Activity 3: Facts versus values

When looking at an issue in depth, it is often useful to check whether the questions being considered are factual or ethical questions. Most issues involve both factual and ethical questions. Distinguishing between the two can help students to clarify their thinking and better organise their investigations.

Factual questions

Factual questions ask about the way things are. They consider the facts, or the objective truth about a situation. By this, we mean those things that are generally agreed, or assumed, to be true. Facts are usually established through observation, although in practice people often rely on the authority of others who have done the observing, since there are too many facts in the world for any one person to establish independently.

How can students answer factual questions? They can:

- make their own observations and conduct experiments
- research other people's observations, or look things up in books or on the internet.

It is important for students to keep thinking critically in order to avoid errors whenever possible. They need to check the validity of their observations, of experimental results and of the sources they take as authoritative.

Ethical questions

Ethical questions ask about the way things should be, and are based on value systems. People ask ethical questions in order to determine how good or bad a situation is, what should be done about it and who should be responsible for it. Students can answer ethical questions by applying the four ethical reasoning perspectives:

- Principles
- Agreements
- Virtues
- Consequences (See Chapter One)

Facts and values are both important. Factual questions help establish a basis of evidence to support decision-making. If people don't know the facts of a situation, they are likely to make decisions based on prejudices and misconceptions, which can produce disastrous consequences. Facts, however, will never produce a response on their own. Ethical questions add motivation and direction to the facts. There is little point in knowing what the likely effects of increasing immigration are, if nobody cares about them. Factual questions help establish where people are. Ethical questions help establish where they want to be. They need to know both where they are and where they want to be in order to decide which way they should go.

Here are some useful guiding questions for considering the factual and ethical dimensions of an issue:

- Which of these questions are factual questions, and which are ethical questions?
- What facts need to be known in order to establish the truth of these statements?
- What are the value questions that should be asked?

Questions of fact	Questions of value
What is Australia's population?	Is there a problem here?
What is our birth rate?	How much is too much? Too little?
How has it changed?	Are there any principles involved?
What relationship does birth rate have to population?	What are the possible consequences?
What factors increase population?	Have any agreements been made?
What factors decrease population?	What would a good society do?
	Does something need to be done here? If so, who should do what?

© 2011 Hawker Brownlow Education • 9781742392547 • HB2547

Sorting the Questions

The following is an example of how students might sort their factual and ethical questions. At the end of this chapter is the Resource Sheet, 'Factual questions versus ethical questions'.

Step 1: Students choose a focus question arising from the Community of Inquiry.

Step 2: Students sort related questions from the Community of Inquiry into two columns.

For example:

Issue:	Australian Population and Resources
Focus question:	Should we increase the rate of immigration to Australia?

<table>
<tr><td colspan="2">Use this sheet to help you sort your questions according to whether they are factual questions or ethical questions.

Remember:
• You may need to break a big question down into a series of smaller, more manageable questions.
• Thinking about one question often leads to another question.
• Behind every ethical question lies a series of factual questions.</td></tr>
<tr><td>Factual questions
What is the situation like?</td><td>Ethical questions
What should the situation be like?</td></tr>
<tr><td>Students' responses might be along the lines of:
What is the current population? How has this changed over time?
What is the current immigration rate?
What effect does the rate of immigration have on population?</td><td>Students' responses might be along the lines of:
What size population should Australia have?
What are our environmental obligations?
What are our obligations to people already living in Australia?
What are our obligations to people living in other countries?</td></tr>
</table>

Step 3: Examine each question to see whether it inspires further questions.

Students might now choose one of three options. The first is to begin their research by trying to find the answers to some of the questions they have recorded. The second is to use these questions to help them broaden their scope of research by following up a different question. The third option is to use these lists to refine their research. They might cross out any question that does not contribute to the core question. They might put aside any information they have gathered that is not directly relevant to the remaining questions.

Activity 4: Misleading statistics

To demonstrate how statistics can be presented and interpreted in misleading ways, we acquired a genuine table from the Australian Bureau of Statistics. It shows the rate of criminal trespass in one Australian state, South Australia. This table is also on the Resource Sheet, 'Misleading statistics'. This table shows the gender breakdown of juveniles accused of serious criminal trespass offences recorded by the South Australian Police, in the financial years 1993–94 and 2002–03.

South Australian Juvenile Serious Criminal Trespass Offences		
	1993–94	**2002–03**
Males	1835	1173
Females	110	110
Persons	1945	1283
Adapted from Australian Institute of Criminology 2002, 'Juvenile Crime and Justice', *http://www.aic.gov.au/publications/rpp/11/ch2.pdf*, accessed 7 Jan 2004, and South Australia Police 2003, 'South Australia Police Annual Report 2002–2003', *http://www. sapolice.sa.gov.au/pdf_file/Annual_Report_2002_03.pdf*, accessed 22 April 2004		

We then concocted an article for a fictitious magazine, *Boyzrule*, claiming that crime by females is rising. In contrast, we concocted an article for a fictitious magazine, *Girlzone*, deploring the crime rate of males. The articles are provided on pages 74.

Statistics can be misleading if we don't consider them carefully. We can fail to notice mistakes or deliberate distortions when we glance briefly at a graph or assume that the source is trustworthy. Thinking critically can help us to identify deliberate or accidental distortions fairly easily. Scales can be distorted by not starting at 0, by having different scales on each axis or by having gaps in the scale. Pictographs can mislead by distorting the area of the pictures used. Inappropriate comparisons can be made, often by using two different data types. And there's also the cliché that 75 per cent of all statistics are made up on the spot.

Useful questions to ask in identifying misleading statistics include:

- What do the statistics presented seem to show?
- What do they actually show?
- What do they not show?
- Is a fair comparison being made?
- Do the statistics presented actually support the claim being made?
- Does the graph make sense?
- Did these statistics come from a trustworthy source?

© 2011 Hawker Brownlow Education • 9781742392547 • HB2547

Set up a 'Dodgy data' or 'Suss statistics' display. Encourage students to find examples of the misleading use of statistics in the media or in their research. Ask students to identify what is wrong with the way the statistics are being used and mount both the example and the critique in the display. This provides the opportunity for further scrutiny and possible challenges, which can spark off even more questions. Students can also engage in their own data distortion, which is an excellent way for them to learn how to distinguish between good and poor quality presentation.

The Resource Sheets are useful for an exercise in identifying misleading statistics. Students can read the fictional articles from *Boyzrule* and *Girlzone* magazines, and compare them with the data provided. Asking the above questions can help them to identify ways in which the data has been distorted. It would be useful for students to graph the relevant data to see how it might appear without distortion.

Here is one example of how such a graph might look.

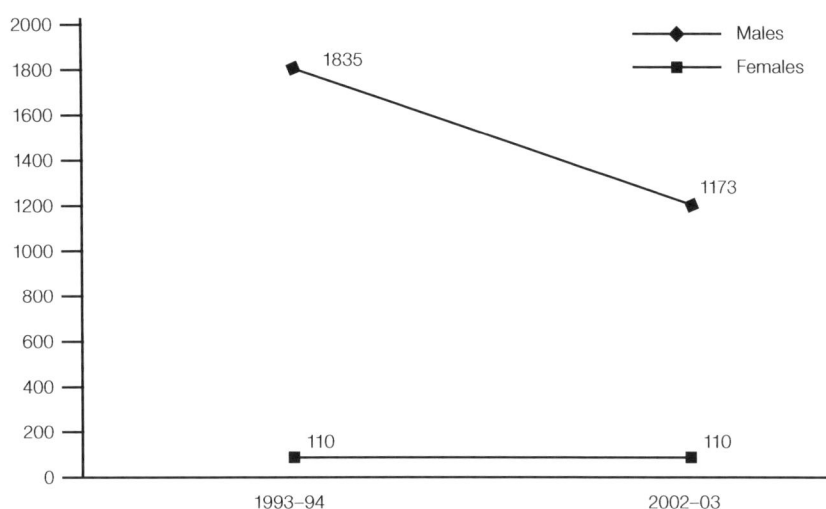

This graph shows that males committed many more of these offences than females, but that the female trend was increasing, while the male trend was decreasing. Both fictional articles show a clear bias in favour of one gender and distort the information from the report to support their own bias. They both use data only from the first category of property offences. Motor vehicle theft, stealing, arson, property damage and fraud are ignored. This was apparently a time-saving measure, but it is important to note that the table may not be representative of all property offences. The articles should not make claims about property crime if they have only considered one type of property crime. This is over-generalisation. Both articles also use loaded terms, such as 'skyrocketed', 'dive', 'always', 'as many as' and 'whopping'. Emotive language can mislead readers even when accurate data is used. The following is a detailed analysis of other distortions within each article.

Boyzrule Magazine: Graphical distortions

The Boy Crime graph shows the absolute number of selected crimes committed by boys, while the Girl Crime graph shows the *percentage* committed by girls, rather than the absolute figures. These percentages were calculated for each period as follows:

Males	
1993–94	2002–03
$\dfrac{1835}{1945}$ $= 0.9434447...$ $\approx 94\%$	$\dfrac{1173}{1283}$ $= 0.9142634...$ $\approx 91\%$
Females	
1993–94	2002–03
$\dfrac{110}{1945}$ $= 0.05655526...$ $\approx 6\%$	$\dfrac{110}{1283}$ $= 0.08573655...$ $\approx 9\%$

Because boys committed fewer of these crimes in 2002–03 than they had in 1993–94, while girls committed the same number of crimes in each period, the boys' percentage fell, forcing the girls' percentage to rise. This is an inappropriate comparison, and a good illustration of how relative statistics can be easily misused. The scale on the Boy Crime graph begins at 1000 and continues to 3000, which moves the points down towards the x-axis and away from the top of the graph, making the variables seem lower than they really are. The scale on the Girl Crime graph begins at 0, but ends at 10 per cent, just above the second variable. This moves the graph up away from the x-axis, making the variables seem higher than they really are. It also makes the rise from 6 per cent to 9 per cent seem bigger than it really is. The scales in both graphs are very small, discouraging readers from examining the figures and identifying the distortions made. These techniques encourage readers to interpret the graphs only from the placement of the points and the slope of each line. This false interpretation supports the *Boyzrule* bias.

Frank Furphy's analysis

Frank identifies a 36 per cent drop in boy crime and a 50 per cent rise in girl crime. These percentages were calculated as follows:

Boys	Girls
$\dfrac{(value_1 - value_2)}{value_1}$ $= \dfrac{1835 - 1173}{1835}$ $= \dfrac{662}{1835}$ $= 0.3607629...$ $\approx 36\%$ drop	$\dfrac{(\%_2 - \%_1)}{\%_1}$ $= \dfrac{(9 - 6)}{6}$ $= \dfrac{3}{6}$ $= 0.5$ $\approx 50\%$ rise

This is another deceptive and invalid comparison between absolute and relative figures to suit *Boyzrule*'s bias.

Girlzone Magazine: Graphical distortions

Girlzone magazine chose a three-dimensional block chart with a very small scale axis. This makes accurate interpretation virtually impossible because the blocks don't match the scale. This chart appears to suggest that boys may have committed more than 2000 of these offences. The blocks are not adequately labelled, so the uninformed reader has no way of knowing that the front of the block shows the later figure while the back of the block shows the earlier figure. Many readers would be unable to draw any conclusions about how the figures had changed over time, and those who tried to would probably conclude that male offences had risen even though they fell.

Dishonest table

The table contains no year headings and reverses the order of the columns from the original data table. This again either totally befuddles the reader, or leads to the conclusion that boy crime rose rather than fell.

Frank Furphy's Analysis

Frank continues the deception by again reversing the order of the statistics quoted, implying a rise instead of a fall. Since we conventionally consider earlier statistics before later statistics, it is deceptive to reverse this order without clearly identifying the reversal. By using the phrase 'as many as', Frank decreases the effect of the year labels used. This is a good example of how the most effective deceptions are often those which are closest to the truth.

Sandy Stirrer's Conclusion

Sandy chooses the earlier, higher figure to illustrate the size of the difference in crimes committed by boys and girls. If she used the more current figure, she could only say boys committed eleven times as many offences as girls. It is deceptive to choose the highest figure available to maximise effect when the general assumption is that the most current figure would be used.

Both articles draw on accurate data but are selective with the truth and distort it so much that it would have been no less honest to simply make up imaginary statistics to support their false claims.

After the students have identified the distortions, they could write unbiased articles of their own, using these statistics appropriately to report on the true picture of juvenile serious criminal trespass offences.

Activity 5: Conducting a survey

This exercise is designed to provide students with the opportunity to explore ethical questions using simple statistical methods. A Resource Sheet, 'Using statistics to consider consequences and reach agreements' is provided at the end of the chapter. This activity has six steps involving survey design and implementation, data analysis and interpretation, as well as an optional extension.

Step 1: Students are required to propose a law/rule/policy to be considered

Examples include:

- Family size should be restricted to no more than two children.
- Immigration should be stopped until our population is reduced to ten million.
- The current immigration rate should be increased.
- Migrants should move to low-population centres.

Ideally, the proposition should be related to the questions explored in the previous activities and be chosen by the students.

Step 2: Students identify the concerned parties, those who would be affected by this proposition

This step encourages students to consider the stakeholders in any given issue, and is based on the presumption that stakeholders should be consulted when decisions are made concerning them. There is room here for discussion about who should be allowed to decide these kind of questions and why, and also about the survey design implications. Do we limit our survey to Australians? Or should we include people overseas who are potential migrants? Is it feasible to include overseas people?

Step 3: Students design and conduct a survey to gauge the opinions of the concerned parties

A Resource Sheet for this activity is at the end of this chapter, entitled 'Using statistics to consider consequences and reach agreements'.

Students use this scale as a guide for weighting the responses to their survey

Rating	Description	Weighting
☺☺☺☺	This will make me ecstatic with joy	4
☺☺☺	This will make me very happy	3
☺☺	This will make me quite happy	2
☺	This will make me mildly content	1
☹	This will slightly displease me	-1
☹☹	This will make me quite unhappy	-2
☹☹☹	This will make me very unhappy	-3
☹☹☹☹	This will fill me with despair	-4

(Adapted from Robinson & Garratt 1996)

Students may use this scale as a guide, and develop their own weighting system, or they may use the scale as given. This weighting system simplifies the process of analysing the data once it is collected.

Step 4: Students collect and analyse their data

Students may design their own data collection table or use the 'Predicted Consequences' Resource Sheet provided at the end of this chapter. The data analysis in this exercise involves recording the frequency of each rating, multiplying the frequency by the weighting and finding the sum of the weighted scores. The ratings are weighted so that there is some balance between strength of opinion and the strength of numbers. In this exercise, the response, 'this will make me ecstatic with joy' is four times as strong as the response, 'this will make me mildly content', so one person indicating the strongest response will produce the same weighted score as four people indicating the weakest response. The positive and negative

© 2011 Hawker Brownlow Education • 9781742392547 • HB2547

weightings will centre the balance on 0. No sitting on the fence is allowed, which is why no responses have a 0 weighting. What is the total weighted score?

Step 5: Students interpret results

A positive score indicates support for the proposition. A negative score indicates rejection of the proposition. The more positive or negative a score is, the stronger the overall preference. A 0 score indicates that there is no preference either way. A 0 score will be achieved by an even mix of positive and negative responses. Students can divide the Total Weighted Score by the number of people surveyed, and refer back to the rating scale to determine the overall response. For example, if the Total Weighted Score for 100 people was 380 then the overall response weighting would be 3.8 (which rounds off to 4), indicating strong support for the proposal. A Total Weighted Score of −120 would indicate mild opposition to the proposal.

Step 6: Students evaluate the statistical validity of their opinion poll

Considerations:

- Representative samples:

  Were those surveyed representative of all of the concerned parties?

  Were all the concerned parties accurately identified?

- Bias in survey design:

  Was the weighting scale fair?

  Were leading questions avoided?

- Interpreting survey results:

  Were appropriate conclusions drawn?

- Opinion versus factual data:

  Did the people surveyed know how they would be affected by the proposition, or were they just guessing?

How appropriate is it to use this kind of information as the basis for making ethical decisions? What other concerns might you have? Can you identify any flaws in this approach? These are open questions which could lead to further investigations, or be briefly discussed to stimulate evaluative thinking.

Extension

Students find, examine and analyse other statistics that might have a bearing on a possible law. What action do the available statistics suggest would result in the greatest good for the greatest number? This extension could be used as a springboard for the following research activity. Alternatively, students might prefer to close off this activity and switch to a different question.

Activity 6: Research project

Students research one or more of the questions, issues or ideas raised during this unit, with an aim of making active recommendations about what should be done and who should be doing it. Many of these ideas are complex enough to engage the whole class in their research. Alternatively students could choose their own areas in which to conduct individual or small group research. The Resource Sheets at the end of this chapter, 'Displaying statistics' and 'Common statistical graphs', provide a quick reference guide to the presentation of statistical information to assist students in their research. 'Structure of a statistical report' offers a framework for reporting their findings.

Activity 7: Unit review and evaluation

It is important for students to present their research findings in a meaningful way, either within the class or to a wider audience, and to reflect on what they have learned throughout the unit. Some peer or self evaluation might be appropriate within this context. This is a useful time to consider together the question of who should do what. It is not sufficient to sit around and say, 'this is how it is', or 'this is how it should be', and then do nothing. If students recommend changes to government policy, they should at least pass those recommendations on to their local Member of Parliament and the relevant government department/s. If they recommend some kind of public education campaign, they should be supported in conducting one. If they recommend changes in the way the media report on these issues, they should pass their recommendations on to the media organisations concerned. If they make recommendations for practical activities, they should be supported in implementing those activities.

Conclusion

The purpose of this book is to provide ethical strategies to enable people of good will to make judgements, come to decisions and negotiate with each other. Specific tools are provided in Chapters One and Two.

Ethical decisions are made in real contexts, where the facts are as vital to the process as the ethical judgements. Facts can be presented by a variety of methods, and the methods used influence people's judgements. In this chapter we encouraged students to consider different statistical presentations of facts, to choose appropriate methods and to be aware that others may choose misleading methods. We hope that the result will be a society in which people can acquire reliable information and apply fruitful ethical strategies to produce good decisions.

Discussion ideas for a Community of Inquiry on Australian population and resources

Tick a position (0 to 10) alongside each of the ideas listed, saying how likely you think it is that the statement is true. Compare responses with your classmates. Then make a list of other statements that you think would produce interesting discussion.

very unlikely very likely	
0 ... 1 ... 2 ... 3 ... 4 ... 5 ... 6 ... 7 ... 8 ... 9 ... 10	
	Australia's population is too low.
	Australia has an ageing population.
	Australia's population is greater than our ecology can handle.
	We need to increase our birth rate.
	We need to increase immigration to Australia.
	We need to increase our standard of living.
	Australia has an ageing population problem.
	Increasing immigration will destabilise Australian society.
	Australia's population is not a problem.
	Increasing immigration will increase unemployment.
	We need to decrease consumption and pollution.
	Increasing immigration will increase demand for goods and services.
	Too many Australians live in big cities.

Factual questions versus ethical questions

Issue:	
Focus Question:	

Use this sheet to help you sort your questions according to whether they are factual questions or moral questions.

Remember:
- You may need to break a big question down into a series of smaller, more manageable questions.
- Thinking about one question often leads to another question.
- Behind every moral question lies a series of factual questions.

Factual questions: What is the situation like?	Moral questions: What should the situation be like?

You can now use these questions to broaden or refine your research.

Misleading statistics

Statistics can be very useful when we analyse them carefully. Unfortunately, sometimes they can be misinterpreted or deliberately distorted to support a particular argument. Thinking critically can help us to identify and avoid misleading statistics.

This table shows the gender breakdown of juveniles accused of serious criminal trespass offences recorded by the South Australian Police in the financial years 1993–94 and 2002–03.

South Australian Juvenile Serious Criminal Trespass Offences		
	1993–94	**2002–03**
Males	1835	1173
Females	110	110
Persons	1945	1283
Adapted from Australian Institute of Criminology 2002, Juvenile Crime and Justice, *http://www.aic.gov.au/ publications/rpp/11/ch2.pdf*, accessed 7 Jan 2004, and South Australia Police 2003, South Australia Police Annual Report 2002-2003, *http://www.sapolice.sa.gov.au/pdf_file/Annual_Report_2002_03.pdf*, accessed 22 April 2004		

Your task:

1. Make an appropriate graph of this data.

2. Considering both the above table and your own graph, analyse (draw appropriate meaning from) the data.

   a What do these statistics seem to show?

   b. What do they actually show?

   c. What do they not show?

3. Evaluate the sources of these statistics. Do you think these sources are trustworthy?

4. Read the fictional articles from *Boyzrule* magazine and *Girlzone* magazine, which were both developed from this data.

5. Examine the articles carefully:

   a. Do their claims match your own data analysis?

   b. Does either of the articles show any kind of bias?

   c. Are the claims they make supported by the original data?

6. Identify as many distortions as you can find in each article.

7. Explain how the data has been distorted.

8. Evaluate the trustworthiness of these two magazines as statistical sources.

Misleading statistics – Articles to examine

Boyzrule magazine

WHO'S BAD? FEMALE CRIME RATE SOARS!

Recent government statistics show that the proportion of juvenile crimes committed by girls has skyrocketed, while boy crime has taken a dive.

South Australian Police statistics indicate that the number of break, enter and stealing offences committed by boys between the ages of 10 and 17 fell by 36% in the last nine years, according to analyst Frank Furphy. 'The proportion of these offences committed by girls jumped by an enormous 50%!' he said.

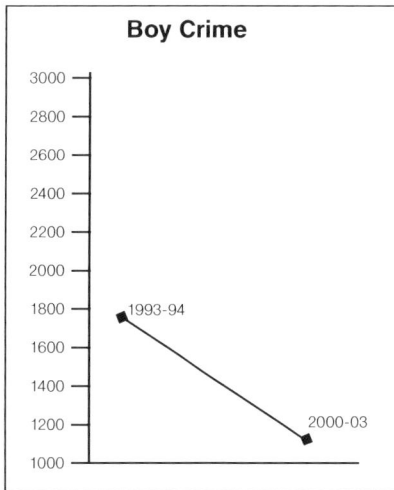

Boy Crime

(graph: y-axis from 1000 to 3000; point at 1993-94 near 1800; point at 2000-03 near 1100)

Activist Sean Stirrer was thrilled with these findings. 'These statistics support what we've been saying all along. It's time the authorities got off our case and paid attention to where it's really needed,' he said, 'They should go after the girls for a change!'

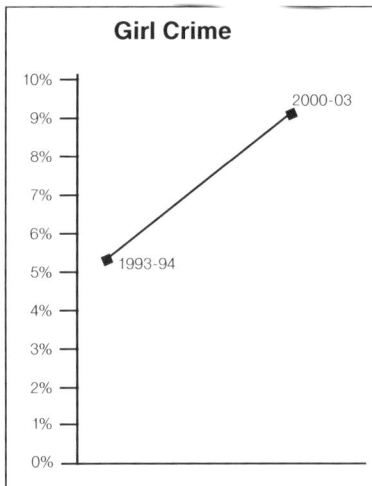

Girl Crime

(graph: y-axis from 0% to 10%; point at 1993-94 near 5%; point at 2000-03 near 9%)

Girlzone magazine

BOY CRIME SKY HIGH!

Boys have always committed much more crime than girls. They still do, and recent government statistics prove it.

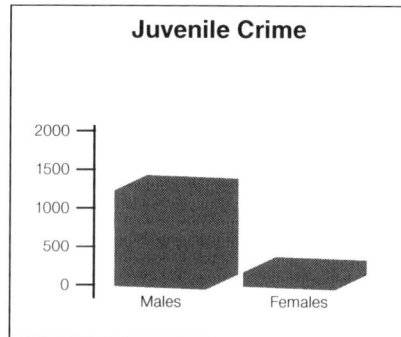

Juvenile Crime

(bar graph: y-axis from 0 to 2000; Males bar near 1300; Females bar near 200)

South Australian Police statistics show that males committed 91% of all juvenile serious criminal trespass offences in 2002–03, and as many as 94% of offences in 1993-94, while the number of crimes committed by girls had remained stable, according to analyst Frank Furphy.

How we compare		
Boys	1173	1835
Girls	110	110

Activist Sandy Stirrer was thrilled with these findings. 'Boys have committed a whopping 17 times as many offences as girls. These figures support what we've been saying all along,' she said, 'Boys are rotten, sleazy criminals!'

© 2011 Hawker Brownlow Education • 9781742392547 • HB2547

Using statistics to consider consequences and reach agreements

A good social policy is one that

- produces good consequences for the people it affects, and
- is agreed to by the people it affects.

Your task:

1. Propose a law/rule/policy to be considered.

2. Identify the concerned parties, those who would be affected by this proposition.

3. Design and conduct a survey to gauge the opinions of the concerned parties. Use this scale as a guide for weighting the responses to your survey:

Rating	Description	Weighting
☺☺☺☺	This will make me ecstatic with joy.	4
☺☺☺	This will make me very happy.	3
☺☺	This will make me quite happy.	2
☺	This will make me mildly content.	1
☹	This will slightly displease me.	-1
☹☹	This will make me quite unhappy.	-2
☹☹☹	This will make me very unhappy.	-3
☹☹☹☹	This will fill me with despair.	-4

(Adapted from Robinson & Garratt, 1996)

4. Collect and analyse your data.

5. Interpret your results. Is your total weighted score positive, neutral or negative? What does this mean? What does your opinion poll suggest is the greatest good for the greatest number? Does your survey indicate that this proposal is one which can be generally agreed upon by the concerned parties? How do you know this?

6. Evaluate the statistical validity of your opinion poll.

- Some issues to consider:
- census versus sample
- representative samples
- bias in survey design
- interpreting survey results
- opinion versus factual data

How appropriate is it to use this kind of information as the basis for making ethical decisions? What other concerns might you have? Can you identify any flaws in this approach?

Extension

Find, examine and analyse other statistics that might have a bearing on your possible law. What action do the available statistics suggest would result in the greatest good for the greatest number?

© 2011 Hawker Brownlow Education • 9781742392547 • HB2547

Predicted consequences

Proposition:				
Rating	Tally	Frequency	Weighting	Weighted Score (Frequency x Weighting)
☺☺☺☺			4	
☺☺☺			3	
☺☺			2	
☺			1	
☹			-1	
☹☹			-2	
☹☹☹			-3	
☹☹☹☹			-4	
		Total Score		

(Adapted from Robinson & Garratt, 1996)

Research project – Displaying statistics

Statistical information can be used within the body of a text or conversation, but displaying this information in a frequency table or graph can present a lot of information in an easy to understand format (Adapted from Lowe, 1988; Abdelnoor, 1979).

Frequency tables present data in rows and columns. They should always have a title, column headings and a data source statement. One column displays the data categories, values or class intervals, and another displays the frequency, or the number of cases fitting each category, value or class interval. They may also contain some elements of data analysis, such as relative frequency (its proportion to the total) or cumulative frequency (the sum of all frequencies up to and including this one).

Population, growth rate and rank, selected countries:

	ESTIMATED POPULATION			PROJECTED POPULATION	RANK	
	2002	2003	Growth rate	2050	2003	2050
Country	million	million	%	million	no.	no.
Australia	19.6	19.9	1.2	26.4	52	65
Canada	31.9	32.2	1.0	41.4	35	42
China	1,279.2	1,287.0	0.6	1,417.6	1	2
India	1,034.2	1,049.7	1.5	1,601.0	2	1
Indonesia	231.3	234.9	1.5	336.2	4	4
Malaysia	22.7	23.1	1.9	43.1	46	41
New Zealand	3.9	4.0	1.1	4.8	121	124
Papua New Guinea	5.2	5.3	2.4	10.7	109	92
Singapore	4.5	4.6	3.5	10.8	115	91
Thailand	63.6	64.3	1.0	74.0	19	23
United Kingdom	59.9	60.1	0.3	64.0	21	29
United States of America	287.7	290.3	0.9	420.1	3	3
World	6,228.6	6,302.5	1.2	9,084.5	. .	. .

(. . = not applicable)
Sources: ABS for Australian estimated and projected populations (Series B); US Bureau of the Census, International Data Base for selected countries and world estimated and projected populations and all rankings. Australian Bureau of Statistics, 2003.

 © 2011 Hawker Brownlow Education • 9781742392547 • HB2547

RESOURCE SHEET

Graphs (also called charts) show statistical information in a pictorial format. Useful graphs include pie charts, bar charts, column charts, histograms, scatter plots, line plots, cumulative frequency graphs, stem and leaf plots, and box and whisker plots.

Data Types

- Categorical

    Without numbers (e.g. nationality, gender)

- Discrete

    Exact (separate) number values (e.g. the numbers on a die: 1, 2, 3, 4, 5 or 6)

- Continuous

    Number values which are part of a continuous measurement scale (e.g. height, speed)

    Note: these values are grouped into class intervals

- Paired

    Tell us two different things about the same subject (e.g. age and gender for immigrants)

    Note: Relationships between paired data may be, but are not always investigated

Research project – Common statistical graphs

Type: Bar/Column Chart

(If the bars are horizontal, it's a bar chart. If they're vertical, it's a column chart.)

Purpose: To show frequencies of categorical or discrete data in relation to each other.

Features of a good graph:

- makes sense
- appropriate title and axis labels
- bars/columns have equal width
- bars/columns don't touch.

Limitations:

- not appropriate for continuous data.

Australian Population Estimates

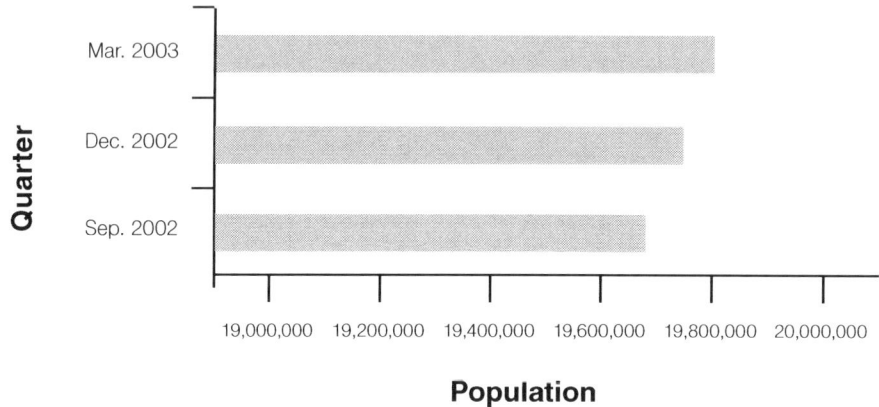

State and Territory Population Estimates

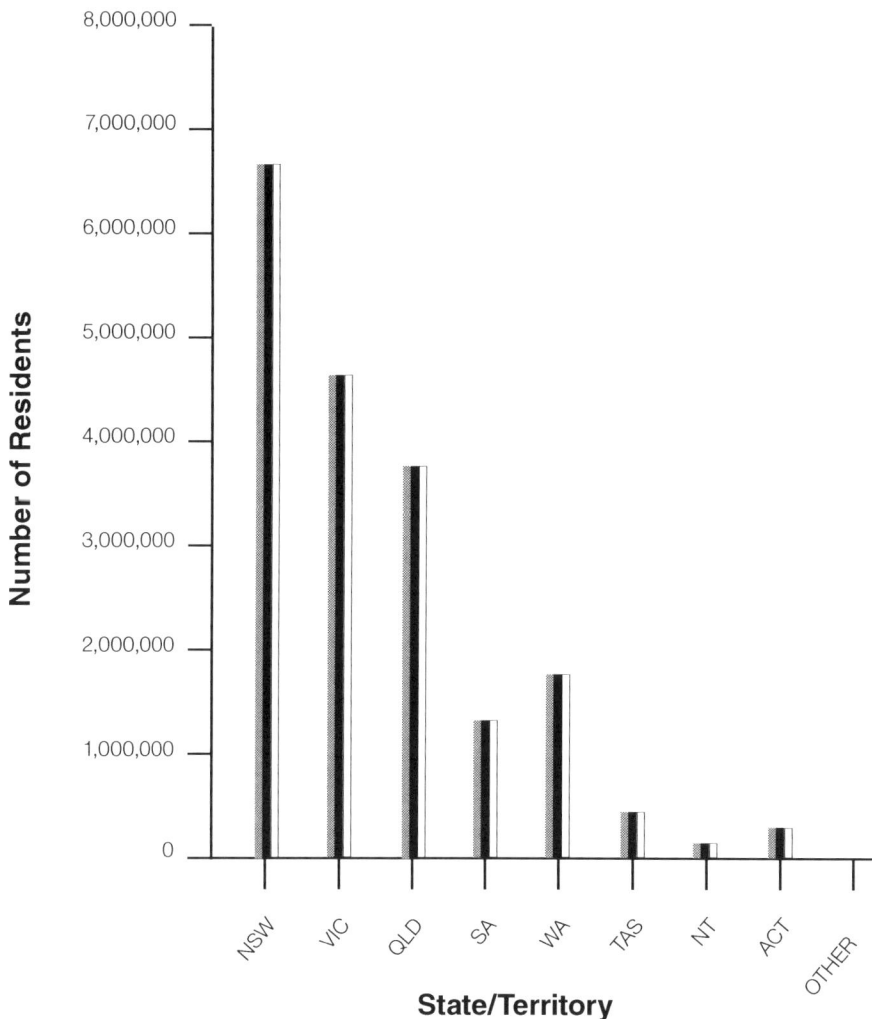

© 2011 Hawker Brownlow Education • 9781742392547 • HB2547

Type: Pie Chart

Purpose: To show relative frequencies as a fraction of a total.

Features of a good graph:

- makes sense
- appropriate title and segment labels
- area of each segment is proportional to the relative frequency it displays.

Limitations:

- only appropriate when the total of all frequencies is meaningful
- hard to read when there are many categories.

Population of Australia States and Territories, March 2003

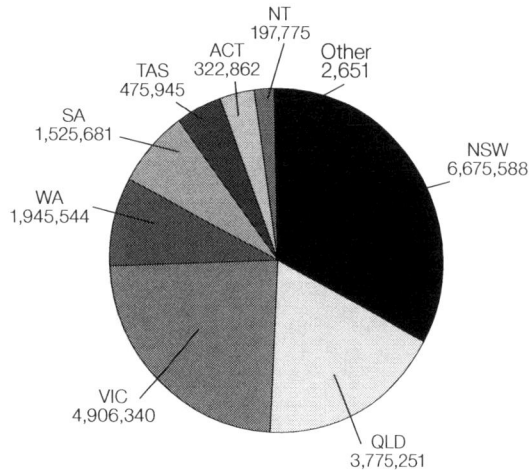

Type: Scatter Plot

Purpose: To show how two variables are related

Features of a good graph:

- makes sense
- appropriate title and axis labels
- clear and appropriate scales.

Limitations:

- needs two variables

  Source: Australian Bureau of Statistics, 3201.0 Population by Age and Sex, Australian States and Territories[1]

Median Age of Population

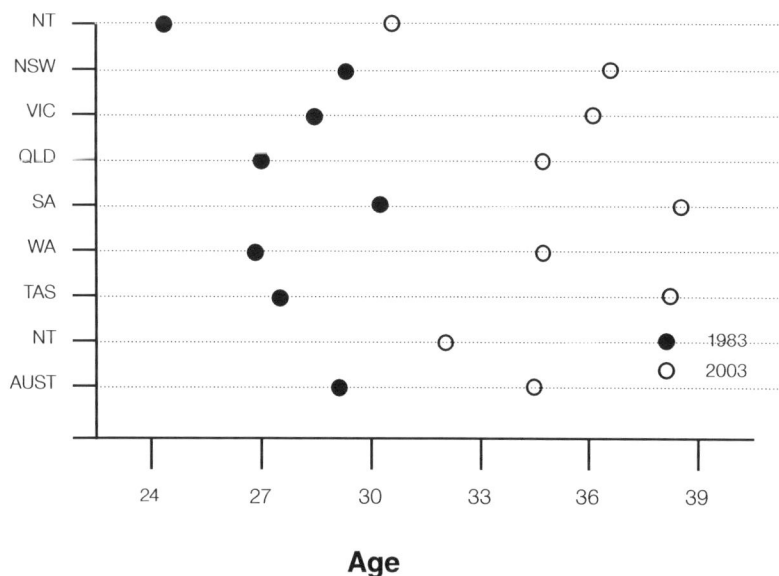

Type: Histogram

Purpose: To show the distribution of continuous data

Australia: 2000

Male

Female

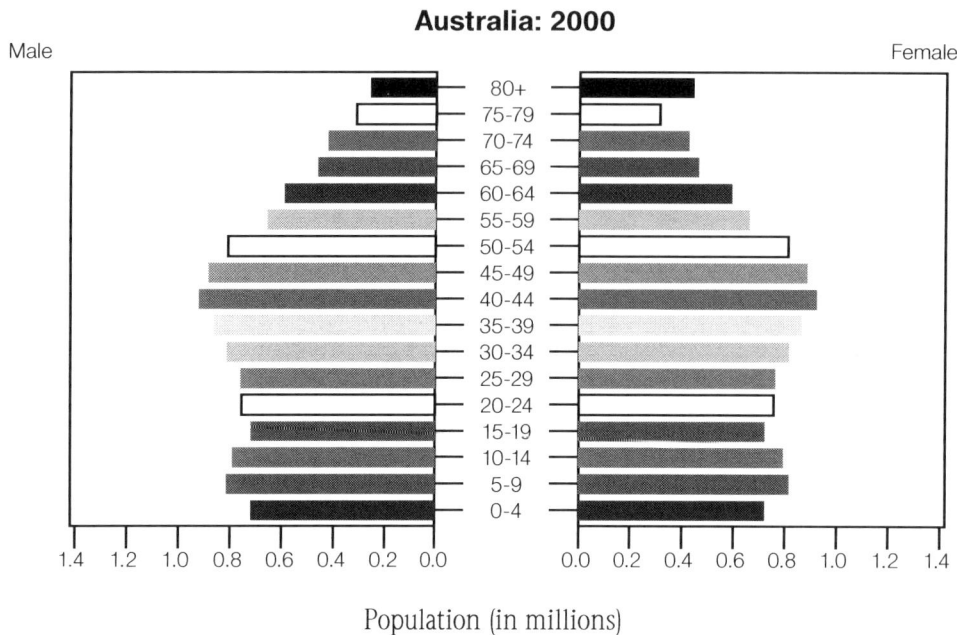

Population (in millions)

Source: U.S. Census Bureau, International Data Base

http://www.census.gov/cgi-bin/ipc/idbsum?cty=AS, accessed 7 January, 2004.

Features of a good graph:

- makes sense
- appropriate title and axis labels
- columns are joined together, just like the class intervals join up
- area of column corresponds to frequency of class intervals
- frequencies are labelled only if the columns have equal width, showing equal class intervals.

Limitations:

- Not appropriate for categorical or discrete data

(Adapted from Lowe, 1988; Simmonds & Silva 2003; Australian Bureau of Statistics 2003; US Census Bureau 2004)

Research project – Guiding questions

Use these questions to help you analyse the data you are working with, and decide whether the data in the explorations will help solve the problem you are working on.

☐ Are there any problems with the way this data is presented and used?

☐ Does this information have a bearing on the problem/question you are working on?

☐ Does this information answer any of your questions?

☐ Is there a problem here?

☐ Does something need to be done about this? If so, who should do what?

☐ Is there a principle involved?

☐ What are the possible consequences?

☐ Has an agreement been made?

☐ What would a good person/government/community do?

Chapter 6

Walking in another's shoes: Active listening and role-play in drama

This chapter provides:

- a rationale for the use of ethical decision-making in drama
- a suggested curriculum unit using the theme of 'identity'
- specific activities for teaching ethics through dramatic activities
- Resource Sheets:

    Role-play

    Scenario role-play

    Writing task

Please note: Chapters One and Two provide essential material about the conduct of ethical decision-making and should be read in conjunction with this chapter. Chapter Eight provides evaluation and assessment tools.

In this chapter, we begin with a rationale explaining the theoretical basis for the use of ethical decision-making in drama. We then suggest specific activities for teaching ethics through dramatic activities, with clear explanations and an emphasis on student reflection. This is important in encouraging autonomy in learning. We thus provide students with definite strategies for solving ethical dilemmas in their lives.

Rationale

In drama it is easy to introduce ethical decision-making in an interesting way that involves participation and movement. The topics, themes and subjects for performance are wide-ranging, and there is a great deal of flexibility available to the teacher. Students enjoy topics which involve issues of relevance to them, and many of these have an ethical basis. For example, should students wear a uniform? Is it right to insist on unquestioning obedience? Should students follow the crowd and steal from supermarkets? Is suicide a solution? It is often useful to choose topical issues from the media or recent school decision-making. Unfortunately, it is common in such discussions that students are not taken any further than to a happy (or frustrating) sharing of their ideas. Providing them with the four strategies for ethical decision-making will allow for a fruitful conclusion through their activities and deliberations (Chapters One and Two). The aim of this chapter is to introduce strategies which students can apply to their decision-making.

- by role-playing different characters, students can better understand opposing viewpoints.
- by understanding the 'four things a reasonable person knows' (page 18), they are able to rationally consider issues together.
- By practising the use of principles, consequences, agreements and virtue in ethical decision-making through examples and role-plays, they are able to recognise their values and apply them to their own decision-making.

A suggested curriculum unit using the theme of identity

Who am i? What is right for me? What is right for others?

The theme of 'identity' is not only an interesting issue for middle school students, but also a very good introduction to the creation of a character. It leads to a depth of understanding of differing viewpoints on issues. At the same time as building their dramatic skills, students are learning about ethical decision-making and adding another dimension to the Community of Inquiry (Chapter Two).

This sequence of lessons begins with an examination of the 'four things a reasonable person knows' so that the group can agree on how to handle discussion. It moves to the self, connecting with the students' interest in the 'big' questions, using role-play and improvisation and then performance as part of the Community of Inquiry. An emphasis is placed on reflection, and ensuring that students recognise the purpose of each activity. This is essential if students are to take control of their own learning, and make connections with the world outside of the classroom. We believe that explicit teaching of thinking strategies is often insufficiently provided. In this chapter, we make explicit some useful activities.

Step 1: A preliminary agreement

Provide students with the Resource Sheet, 'four things a reasonable person knows', from Chapter Two. The items should be discussed and agreement reached on their implementation. Students should glue this into their books or folders for easy reference. Thus, in later disputes about behaviour or purpose, anyone in the group can refer back to the agreement reached.

Step 2: The discussion starter

Community of Inquiry using a number line

Choose a simple question first. For example, 'Who thinks it is a good idea to keep pets?' or 'Should students have to wear school uniform?' A list of discussion ideas follows. One way to get discussion going is to get students moving, and the number line is a great tool with which to do this. One corner of the room represents 'yes', or the number 10, while the other represents 'no', or 0. The line between the two represents all the numbers in between.

(no) 0 ——————————— 5 (on the fence) ——————————— 10 (yes)

By asking questions which require yes or no answers, the teacher can ask students to move to their positions on the number line without talking. Discussion comes later, and they should be expected to make their own decisions at this time.

Step 3: Discussion

Once students are on the line, choose two students who hold differing positions and ask them to justify their position. Perhaps they can have a conversation and ask each other questions about their decision, leading to more discussion. Let others join in, one at a time. Encourage the students to listen and carefully consider their positions. Reinforce the 'four things a reasonable person knows' in this activity by giving them the opportunity to change positions. Give the first student to move a reward of some kind. Then try moving a student (A) alongside one with an opposing view (B). A explains B's viewpoint to the class, and cannot stop until B is satisfied.

Reflection

Ask students, 'What learning is taking place here?' Communication skills, quick thinking, presentation of argument and, most importantly, good listening skills all apply here. Discuss the importance of really listening to other viewpoints, rather than just thinking of what they are going to say next, and reconsidering their position on an issue. This is one of the key points in the Community of Inquiry, which is clearly demonstrated by this exercise.

Step 4: Deeper discussion of identity questions

Using the number line, ask questions such as the following on the topic of identity.

- Who are you? Are you your name? If you think you are totally your name, move to the number 10 position.
- If you think yes/no, move to number 5.
- Are you your hair?
- If you lost all your hair, would you still be you?
- If you had an operation on your brain, would you still be you?
- Are you the same person you were when you were three? Thirteen? Last week?
- Will you be the same person when you are 40 or 80?

Encourage every student to speak so that they are each a part of the discussion. Students should have their conversations with each other, rather than using the teacher as a conduit. Use the number line to discuss the need to value each other's opinion, as much as the teacher's. The classroom atmosphere should allow students to be comfortable and enjoy moving their positions.

- Do you want others in the group to value your opinion?

Introduce or remind students of the importance of body language, such as eye contact, turning their body towards the speaker, responding with facial expressions and so on. Ask about different aspects, or an overall question such as: 'Who would like the group to use active listening skills while we are discussing issues? Would you like each person in the group to respond to your ideas with supportive body language?'

Reflection

It then becomes easy to remind the group that they have already agreed to participate in this way if they forget, dismiss each others' ideas or do not listen to others. Students here are not only learning about their own identity, but also about how to work more effectively in a group.

© 2011 Hawker Brownlow Education • 9781742392547 • HB2547

Step 5: Developing dramatic skills through role-play

A simple warm-up

Students choose to be one of the following, and then walk around the room as if they are.

- a famous tennis player who is here for a tournament and aware that everyone knows them as they walk down the street
- a woman who has lost her confidence as a result of losing her job
- a young person who is out to impress his or her friends with their clothing or appearance
- someone who has shoplifted and is feeling guilty as they walk through the checkout

Get half of the class to show the other, and then swap roles and groups. Students could try to identify which role the others are playing.

Reflection

We are unique. We can recognise others from across a school yard, or discern a person's mood and status simply by the way they walk.

Step 6: Exchanging viewpoints on an issue – Duologues

Students form pairs, with one designated A and one B. Choose common student/parent/ teacher disagreements, for example: 'Mum, can I borrow the car tonight?', 'It's not fair, why do I always have to … ?', 'Why didn't you tell me this before?', 'Do I have to … ?', 'But I don't want to go to …', 'Why does it matter what shoes I wear, or whether my shirt is tucked in?' The As begin and the Bs respond, establishing their identity within the first exchange. Roles are then reversed. As with all improvisation work, students need to accept and extend rather than block the exchange, so that the conversation flows. After a few rehearsals to build confidence, ask for demonstrations.

Reflection

Discuss the characters, and the success of each role-play. Are they real? Do your parents behave like that? Is it a believable scene? Depending on the quality of the performances and the age of the students, give them more starter questions and encourage them to go for longer, developing the characters and their viewpoints. Use one or two characters to demonstrate. Allow a role-play to keep going so that as a group, they can delve into the feelings of each character. Return to the earlier lesson's discussion about body language and how it influences reactions of people to each other. Relate to real-life situations, and to how it feels to be in someone else's shoes. Return to the idea of the 'four things a reasonable person knows'. How did students feel when B did not listen to A? Find examples in the role-play of two different viewpoints. Lead into a discussion about the importance of respect for other people's viewpoints, and the need to listen carefully to others so that they know where the other is coming from. Students should practise reversing the roles.

Step 7: Applying 'Four ways of thinking about ethics' (see Chapter One)

Discuss other issues of relevance to the students, such as recent school or media disputes, or other topical issues. Ask students to role-play a discussion, taking the different viewpoints as if they are the characters involved. A Resource Sheet 'Role-play for groups of 5' is provided. Make sure students are familiar with the details of the situation. Introduce the ideas of principles, consequences, virtue and agreements, and discuss their use in ethical decision-making (see Chapter One). Students should then discuss the issue from the four different viewpoints. For example, they can adopt the position of a consequentialist. When the teacher signals to do so, students should change positions and argue with reference to basic principles.

They could be required to stay in character, but add another dimension to their personalities – that of the ethical position they would take.

For example, the father might judge things based on consequences: 'As long as no one gets hurt then everything is okay.' The teacher might use agreements to make judgements: 'You agreed to wear a uniform when you first came to this school.'

The student might use principles to make a decision about their behaviour: 'It's not right that we are not allowed to be treated as individuals.' The grandparent might use virtue when making a decision: 'It's important to be brave and strong and never complain.' Students can then become a group of ethicists and discuss the issue, weighing up all four views. As with balancing a budget, they should then attempt to make a final decision based on the relative strength of the information presented. Students could also become other characters trying to make a decision, with the four ethical schools of thought being presented by friends, family, enemies or advisors. Use whatever works best in the role-play. They should explain the basis upon which they made their final decision. Perhaps, for example, the consequentialist was convincing, but was outweighed by the principles involved, particularly when the agreements also reinforced the principles. A good result would be one where the four views complement each other.

Step 8: Conducting well-informed discussion through research

Select a situation which involves a little research. It may be a dispute between two countries, or two parties in a court case reported in the media. Students need to research the characters' or countries' viewpoints or positions on the issue before presenting their role-play. Students representing one country could attempt to persuade another country to change its view. Take the four ethical viewpoints and match them to the countries concerned, helping the United Nations to make the final decision by balancing these objectively.

Reflection

Ask students to reflect on the lesson or group of lessons. Does it help to role-play so that they can empathise with another's position? Is this a tool they might use in a Community of Inquiry so that they can look more deeply at the differing positions about an issue? What skills have they learned here which relate to drama? Which skills go beyond the subject of drama and into life, decision-making and ethics? Can they use the 'Four ways of thinking about ethics' with ease now?

Step 9: Scenario role-play

See the Resource Sheet, 'Scenario Role-play – Groups of 4'. Students form groups of four. One group becomes the Guardian Angels, representing the four ethical schools of thought. While the other groups rehearse, the Guardian Angels choose, clarify and discuss their ethical viewpoints. Each individual must argue their position based on consequences, agreements, principles or virtue. They should stay with their viewpoint at all times. After reading and watching the following role-play, they should be prepared to present their viewpoint to the class. All other groups are to rehearse the following role-play. At least two groups will be chosen to perform to the class.

The situation

Two parents go out for the night, leaving their 13-year-old son, John, to baby-sit his 8-year-old sister, Jess. John is told not to have friends over, but Susie rings. John cannot resist her pleas to come over to discuss a problem they have, which needs to be resolved that night. Susie says she will tell his school friends an embarrassing secret about him if he doesn't let her come over. John asks his sister to keep quiet and not to tell their parents that Susie came over. Jess agrees to do as he asks, as long as he gives her some of his pocket money. He gets angry and starts pushing her, just as the parents return home.

Students should talk about the situation from all of the characters' viewpoints. In groups, they should take on each role and swap with each other. In addition, there are the roles for the four Guardian Angels, who have been appointed to discuss each of the four ethical schools of thought.

Written Task

Each student is to weigh up the 'four ways of thinking about ethics' to help decide what Jess should do. They should then exchange their final decisions, and see whether the process helped make an ethical decision easier.

Step 10: Thinking, writing and discussing in a Community of Inquiry

The issue to be considered could be, 'Homework: Is it necessary?' Students examine the issue using 'four ways of thinking about ethics', such as:

- Consequences: No success in the long term since work is not retained in the long-term memory; a poor mark when work is not handed in.
- Virtue: Good students always do the right thing and keep up with their work.
- Agreements: The school expects, and students agree, that they will complete the work set by teachers, otherwise penalties will be imposed.
- Principles: Everyone should do his or her best; students have the right to choose not to work hard all the time.

Step 11: Production of a written stance on the issue

See the Resource Sheet. Conduct a Community of Inquiry on the issue. Students can use role-play during the inquiry, to develop an understanding of the issues involved. After the discussion, they may change positions and explain who or what made them do so, in as much detail as they can.

Other Dramatic Resources

Many films deal with issues of identity, for example: *The Net*, *The Matrix* (M15+) and *Bicentennial Man*.

Role-play – Groups of five

The Situation

A student is in trouble at school because they consistently have their shirt out and avoid tucking it in at every opportunity. They have a discussion with the people specified below, carefully considering all viewpoints. The student will make their final decision based on the relative strength of the information presented, as with balancing a budget.

Choose a number from 1 to 5 and 'become' the character that corresponds with the number you have selected. Develop the role-play, but remember that your character must maintain and elaborate on the ethical position stated below.

---

1. The father: judges things based on consequences

e.g. 'There are good reasons for having a school uniform. It helps students to feel part of the school community, and it also stops rich kids showing off their expensive clothes and putting down poor kids. Rebelling against the uniform rules just causes conflict for no good result'

2. The teacher: makes decisions based on agreements

e.g. 'You agreed to wear a uniform when you first came to the school. Even though you did not sign it, it is written in the school diary and is part of the school's expectations. By coming here, you agree to it.'

3. The grandparent: makes decisions based on virtue

e.g. 'It's important to be brave and strong and never complain. Then, you just get on with it and obey the rules without faltering. You'll find out later that it is all about character-building.'

4. Another student: uses principles to make decisions

e.g. 'It's not right that we are not treated as individuals in this school. You don't want to be the same as everyone else, and you should have the right to express yourself and be different if you want to.'

5. The decision-making student: listen to all viewpoints and consider their positions

You may ask questions of each character, asking them to expand as much as possible so that you can make a sensible and well-considered judgement. Explain on what basis you made the final decision. The best decision is one where the four views complement each other.

Scenario role-play – Groups of four

Divide into groups of four. One group becomes the Guardian Angels, representing the four ethical schools of thought. While the other groups rehearse, the Angels choose, clarify and discuss your ethical viewpoint. Each of you must argue your position based on either consequences, agreements, principles or virtue. Stay with your viewpoint at all times. After reading and watching the following role-play, be prepared to present your viewpoint to the class. All other groups rehearse the following role-play. At least two groups will be chosen to perform to the class.

The Situation

A single parent, Jo, goes out for the night leaving their 11-year-old son, John, to baby-sit his 8-year-old sister, Jess. John is told not to have friends over, but his friend, Susie, rings. John cannot resist her pleas to come over and discuss a problem they have which needs to be resolved that night. Susie says she will tell his school friends an embarrassing secret about him if he doesn't let her come over. John asks his sister to keep quiet and not tell the parent that Susie came over. Jess says she will do as he asks, as long as he gives her some of his pocket money. He gets angry and starts pushing her, just as Jo returns home.

Discussion

Your teacher will facilitate the discussion, but ideally the Angels should lead it. Which character is most ethically correct or incorrect in this situation? Why? What should Jess do? The class can ask questions of the characters or of the Angels.

Written task

Write an argument from the point of view of one, two or three of the characters in the scenario. Make sure you use the 'four ways of thinking about ethics' to justify their decision-making. Use any discussion points raised in the class and discussed by the four Angels as well as your own ideas (300 words). Compare your written ideas with your group (100 words).

Did the process (having the role-play, the Angels and the discussion) help your understanding? Could you use or adapt this process, at another time, when making your own decisions? Write about how you might do this. (100 words).

Written task – Is homework necessary?

Examine this issue using the 'four ways of thinking about ethics' as a tool. Write a balanced view of the topic, stating the case for each view before coming to a conclusion.

Criteria for assessment

You will be assessed on your ability to:

- record the four different viewpoints on the topic

- make a judgement using these as a basis for your opinion

- expand on your ideas so that your writing is logical and supported with evidence

- write at least 400 words on the topic

- write with attention to grammar, including spelling and paragraphs.

© 2011 Hawker Brownlow Education • 9781742392547 • HB2547

Chapter 7

Off the classroom wall and out into the world – Moving from static projects to active citizenship in society and environment programs

This chapter provides:

- a rationale for a participatory discussion approach to the teaching of society and environment
- a suggested curriculum unit on the 'Australian goldfields'
- Resource Sheets:

  A Community of Inquiry about social ideas

  A Community of Inquiry on questions specific to the goldfields

  Student assignments

Please note: Chapters One and Two provide essential material about the conduct of ethical decision-making and should be read in conjunction with this chapter. Chapter Eight provides evaluation and assessment tools.

A rationale for a participatory discussion approach

When it comes to civics and citizenship, teachers could adopt an approach that aims only to teach students to be law abiding and public-spirited. We might focus on training our students for future citizenship, and perhaps ensuring that they 'toe the line' in our school community. We could teach them how our society works, about our democratic system, the different levels of government and the history of democracy in Australia. Or, we could adopt a more expansive approach that views students as integral members of our society. We could treat children as valued and valuable citizens now, who have real rights and responsibilities. While we may recognise that they are not completely autonomous and self-determining, we nevertheless realise that children are developing these capacities, and that it is our job to support this. This means that students learn about democracy not only from history books, but also from how they are treated in schools.

American teachers found that the first option by itself does not work. The American study, 'Whereas the People' (Civics Expert Group, 1994), showed that the way we run our schools, rather than what we teach in them, determines the level of citizenship displayed by students. It reported that civic courses, instituted by schools to counter student apathy and anti-social attitudes, made minimal impact on their own. It was only when schools became models of what they espoused that educators saw improvement. Additionally, researchers have found that there is a direct correlation between moral development and student participation. This comes as no surprise: actions speak louder than words.

So how can we encourage student participation in democratic communities? We can set up structures for the student voice, such as class meetings and student councils. But these alone won't do. Without the skills to use these structures effectively, students will abandon them. They will reject them if they sense 'adultism' at work: teachers using these as forums for pushing their own agenda, or that of the school. And they will ignore them if they don't focus on issues they consider relevant, such as school rules that they consider unreasonable. Adults, incidentally, are just the same. They show more interest in issues than in planning events. Fewer teachers would choose to attend a meeting to organise a fundraiser or a school event than one that focused on a relevant issue, such as behaviour management. So, if there are issues that command interest, people need the skills to deal with them. In this chapter we present an approach to teaching a society and environment program that enables students to develop the knowledge, capacities and dispositions to deal with issues. These are the fundamental requirements of ethical citizenship. In order to nurture this ethical citizenship, teachers need to provide their students with three requisites:

- Knowledge within a moral framework.
- Skills to think effectively about the information.
- Encouragement to value and care for the welfare, rights and dignity of others.

In order for moral growth to occur, and in order to become active citizens, students need more than just a desire to be ethical. Ideally, students must have access to information, they must think effectively about what they find out, they must feel strongly about an issue and, then, they must choose what action to take as a result of their inquiry. If children are simply finding and regurgitating information they are wasting time. Most of this information will be outdated or eventually forgotten. Students must make links between facts and concepts, and they must use a moral framework when examining information. If children are not exercising critical discernment of information, then they may well absorb jingoistic fervour and even prejudice. Students must clarify values, including their own, using the tools of critical inquiry. If they are simply carrying out the wishes of their teacher, such as when they visit a home for the elderly or help out with Meals on Wheels, then this could well be a case of the right action for the wrong reasons. Doing the right thing out of convenience or expediency does not develop a moral person. Students must choose their actions. Finally, this approach does not dilute or detract from the objectives of the disciplines that contribute to a society and environment program.

Combining a desire to be ethical with the skills of how to be ethical, we now outline an approach to teaching a society and environment topic that maintains the integrity of the discipline of history, while at the same time addressing the need to nurture civic-minded children.

A suggested curriculum unit

Requisite 1: Students examine a topic in a moral framework

- Identify some key ethical concepts.
- Structure the study into significant focus areas.
- Develop guiding questions centred on the key concepts.
- Direct student assignments towards the guiding questions
- Initiate a Community of Inquiry centred on a particular concept, using narratives and individual accounts of incidents.

Requisite 2: Students learn skills to think effectively about the information. Teach students to identify and use the four frameworks of ethical reasoning:

- Principles
- Consequences
- Agreements
- Virtues

Requisite 3: Teachers encourage students to value and care about the well-being of people and the environment, and to choose to take some action as a result of their study.

Australian goldfields: Curriculum Unit Plan

Requisite 1: Students examine the topic in a moral framework

Step 1: Identify some key ethical concepts

This study could focus on ethical concepts like human rights, justice, equality, liberty, fairness, power, interdependence and sustainability (exploitation of resource and its impact on the environment).

Step 2: Structure the study into significant focus areas

When teachers identify key concepts of a study, it is more likely that they will select significant focus areas so that learning time is fruitful. The whole study might be sequenced into four parts:

- That lucky strike: The lure of gold.
- A long and dangerous trip: Getting to the goldfields.
- Tents, trials and tempers: Getting along and surviving on the goldfields.
- Unrest and uprising: From licence hunts to the Eureka Stockade.

Step 3: Develop guiding questions centred on the key concepts

Initially, the teacher will need to direct much of this questioning, but it does not take children long to learn how to formulate philosophical questions. These questions will then direct investigations and discussions. Notice that the sample questions raised in the Community of Inquiry are more significant than those usually researched by students.

Step 4: A Community of Inquiry about social ideas

A Community of Inquiry is applicable to both the general questions all societies face and to questions specific to the goldfields (see Chapter Two). A Resource Sheet of this activity is included.

Students tick a position (0 to 10) alongside each of the ideas listed, saying how much they agree with the statement. Putting a tick in the far left position, near 1, means strong disagreement. Alternatively, they might have a middle position, or they might strongly agree and tick a position near 10.

strongly disagree strongly agree	
0 ... 1 ... 2 ... 3 ... 4... 5 ... 6 ... 7 ... 8 ... 9 ... 10	
	People are basically greedy
	It is a bad idea for different cultures to live close together.
	People should be treated equally
	Violence is sometimes necessary and justified
	Revolutionaries have no rights.

© 2011 Hawker Brownlow Education • 9781742392547 • HB2547

Step 5: A Community of Inquiry on questions specific to the goldfields

A Resource Sheet of this activity is included. Discussion of the historical issue can be connected by the teacher to contemporary issues.

- When examining the initial rush to the goldfields:

  Are people basically greedy?

  Contemporary connection: the gambling bug.

- When looking at the variety of nationalities represented on the goldfields:

  Is it good for different cultures to live close together? What cultural practices on the goldfields were unjust, unfair or unsustainable?

  Contemporary Connection: distinction of cultures by suburbs in Australia. Link to modern racial conflicts, for example in Bosnia, East Timor or Sri Lanka.

- When looking at the political, economic and social system of the 1850s as evident on the goldfields:

  Were the miners loyal to Australia? Was it right that only those who owned land could vote and enter parliament? Who should have held these rights? Are there certain rights that everyone should have? Are there certain rights applicable to certain groups? What responsibilities/duties should the miners have had? What makes a good citizen? Should only good citizens have a say in the decision-making process? What makes a good leader?

  Contemporary connection: Who has the most say in our school? Why is this so? Should everyone have equal say? Should everyone have equal rights? How can we ensure that minority groups are represented? What responsibilities should those in power have towards those less powerful? And what about others?

- When looking at the Eureka Stockade:

  Was the Eureka Stockade a waste of lives, resources and effort? When is violence necessary? Are there real alternatives?

  Contemporary connection: How do we show our frustrations at those more powerful? What are some effective ways of having our say and getting what we want? How should we express our democratic rights? What are the roles of conflict and dissent in a democracy? How should we express dissent? How can we ensure freedom of speech and, at the same time, protect the rights of other citizens?

These questions are relevant to students' lives both now and in the future. The questions focus on issues, and it is issues that inherently engage the interest of people. This type of question is more likely to command students' interest than the questions they have traditionally researched.

The practice of giving students a choice of multiple activities centred on the topic is questionable. Teachers have to decide how much time they allocate to activities, such as having students make dioramas of the goldfields, period costumes, food and the like, in comparison to time spent focusing on the above issues. Teachers must determine the purpose of the work they give to students, and how much time such activities deserve, given that they are only the means to greater ends, such as the key concepts.

This does not mean that students should only think, talk and write. Tasks that appeal to various learning styles and intelligences can, at the same time, focus student attention on key concepts and guiding questions as shown next.

Step 6: Direct student assignments towards the guiding questions

As the class works through the structure of the study, the teacher carefully designs tasks that will assist them in dealing with the guiding questions. For example, when they examine the Eureka Stockade, their teacher might construct a menu of student tasks that focuses on the conflict. A Resource Sheet of these assignment tasks follows this chapter.

- In any format you like, present the various incidents that led to the ultimate conflict between the authorities and the government. You may choose to present a series of dramatic scenes, such as a wall calendar, ballad, graph or temperature chart of various parties involved in the dispute.
- After investigating the benefits and disadvantages of the gold licence system, devise a fair system for raising revenue.
- Raffaello Carboni is suspected of cowardice. After reading his account of the events leading up to the stockade and to the actual battle itself, determine if he deserves this label. Perhaps organise a debate on this topic with other students.
- Examine the events that led to the battle on 5 December. If you were Peter Lalor, would you have done things differently? Present your decision in any format you wish.

Examine the ways in which people that may have previously competed and conflicted with each other cooperated in the battle. Present a graphic organiser that compares what happened in the 1850s to what happens today, in a strike for example. Notice that we have not invited students to build a model of the stockade, or to design soldiers' or miners' costumes. In the tasks outlined, all work is directed toward a significant end, and engages students in thinking about and defending ethical positions. A philosophical approach doesn't have to always be 'heavy', and can accommodate a range of intellectual abilities and learning preferences.

Step 7: Initiate a Community of Inquiry centred on a particular concept, using narratives and individual accounts of incidents

Stories are an effective way to start a Community of Inquiry session (see Chapter Four). This could expand to include accounts of incidents from primary sources, articles, novels or videos such as Chips Rafferty's *Eureka Stockade*. During this, students could think of questions and issues they would like to discuss, while the teacher records their questions. Then, armed with insight into the students' thinking, the teacher could prepare discussion plans and exercises to guide the inquiry towards significant areas of thought. While the discussion may not head in exactly the direction planned, this initial planning will ensure that the conversation doesn't aimlessly wander.

Community of Inquiry sessions will occur at different times during the study of particular aspects of the history. A video and an account of Scobie's death may prove an excellent introduction to the students' work on conflict. Alternatively, it may be more useful part of the way through or at the end. The astute teacher monitors students' thinking and learning needs, and schedules accordingly. What is most important is that the teacher has initially planned for the use of these resources at some time, and that they know the purpose they might serve in meeting the aims of the study.

Requisite 2: Students learn skills to think effectively about the information

As students investigate various issues relating to the goldfields, and as they seek facts and opinions from a range of materials, they need to be taught the skills of critical inquiry. There are numerous critical thinking resources on the market that teachers can use as references when constructing their own exercises based on the guiding questions they want their students to examine. As students learn to discern bias and prejudice, to differentiate between facts and assumptions, and to look for multiple perspectives on events, they must also develop

© 2011 Hawker Brownlow Education • 9781742392547 • HB2547

an awareness of their own values and dispositions.

Step 8: Teach students to identify and use the four frameworks of ethical reasoning

In Chapter One, we provide 'four ways of thinking about ethics'. It is important that students learn that a person's choice of framework can significantly affect the judgements they make. Judgement might be made against a set of principles, by considering the consequences, within community expectations or by reference to the actions of virtuous characters.

The Eureka Stockade situation is a fine example. When deciding whether the conflict was worthwhile, a consequential perspective would focus on the outcomes of the battle, both at the time and later. A principled view, on the other hand, might measure the results against notions of human rights or non-violence. The person who adopts a social agreement perspective would try to ascertain whether options for negotiation were sufficiently pursued, while someone operating from a framework of virtues would be looking for evidence of courage, honour and compassion. As well as an awareness of one's own leaning towards a particular framework, students also benefit by learning to use all four. Here are some examples of how these might be used:

- A consequentialist framework of ethical reasoning:

  When considering the situation of different cultures coming together, students might look at all of the outcomes of different races mixing or segregating, and nominate what best facilitates inter-racial harmony.

  When looking at the battle, students might weigh up immediate outcomes, such as the deaths and injuries, against the long-term gain of a more democratic governance of the miners.

- A principled framework of ethical reasoning:

  With this perspective, students would focus on the rules and principles they know should guide action. When considering the Eureka Stockade, students might look at the principle of integrity. They might investigate whether Raffaello Carboni did his 'duty' when he avoided taking part in the battle. In the process of this discussion, they would learn that moral action or 'doing the right thing' requires choice. When looking at the political, social and economic conditions on the goldfields, students might examine whether people were being treated with equal respect. Principles also grow from treating others as having an intrinsic value as people, and not as means to ends.

  Concepts like human rights, liberty, equality and power all urge this fundamental understanding of respect for others. Inevitably, students will encounter a clash of principles, such as familial duty versus liberty. Students need to decide whether the miners did 'the right thing' when they fought for their cause, despite knowing that their deaths would leave their wives and children destitute. This can then lead to valuable discussion about the student's own families, and about their parents' responsibilities.

- A social agreement perspective of ethical reasoning:

  When looking at life on the goldfields, at the interactions between the various cultures, and at the conflict between the authorities and the miners, students could devise codes of conduct that would most effectively satisfy everyone. The aim of a perspective of social agreements is to arrive at a win/win situation, where all parties have at least some of their needs met. It involves the skill of negotiation and good management.

  Instructing some students to adopt various roles, and then encouraging others to resolve conflicts, is a worthwhile way to examine the guiding questions centred on these topics.

- A virtues perspective of ethical reasoning:

  When looking at the lure of gold, students might consider why men abandoned their jobs, wives and families for the promise of a lucky strike in the goldfields. They might contrast this with acts of courage, charity and compassion, or their opposites, to determine whether they think humans are inherently good, or inherently selfish and aggressive.

Requisite 3: Teachers encourage students to value and care about the well-being of people and the environment, and to choose to take some action as a result of their study

Ultimately, we want students, as a result of their study, to 'act as ethical, analytical, independent critical thinkers and active citizens' (SACSA: 354). The approach outlined in this chapter assists children to develop moral emotions and capacities. We constantly invite and challenge students to assess and re-assess their values and perspectives about situations, while giving them the skills to form sound opinions and to make valuable decisions. When we focus on ethical concepts, issues that relate to the welfare of people or the preservation of the environment, we ensure that children are encouraged to feel strongly and motivated to act.

The projects on poster-size card that present the 'cut and paste' efforts of students have reached their use-by-date. Hopefully, new curriculum imperatives to make studies in society and environment a more powerful force in shaping the minds and hearts of our children will cause teachers to shift their focus from topics and information gathering, to concepts and critical inquiry, and from static project work to active citizenship. Then, and only then, will we see the natural emergence of considerate, caring and civic-minded children.

A Community of Inquiry about social ideas

Tick a position (0 to 10) alongside each of the ideas listed, saying how much you agree with the statement. Putting a tick in the far left position, near 0, means you disagree strongly. Alternatively, you might have a middle position, or you might strongly agree and tick a position near 10.

strongly disagree strongly agree	
0 ... 1 ... 2 ... 3 ... 4 ... 5 ... 6 ... 7 ... 8 ... 9 ... 10	
	People are basically greedy.
	It is a bad idea for different cultures to live close together.
	People should be treated equally.
	Violence is sometimes necessary and justified.
	Revolutionaries have no rights.

A Community of Inquiry on questions specific to the goldfields

Tick a position 0 to 10 indicating whether you disagree or agree.

When examining the initial rush to the goldfields:

People are basically greedy.

strongly disagree   strongly agree

0 ... 1 ... 2 ... 3 ... 4 ... 5 ... 6 ... 7 ... 8 ... 9 ... 10

When looking at the variety of nationalities represented on the goldfields, think about what cultural practices were unjust, unfair or unsustainable.

It is not good for different cultures to live close together.

strongly disagree   strongly agree

0 ... 1 ... 2 ... 3 ... 4 ... 5 ... 6 ... 7 ... 8 ... 9 ... 10

When looking at the political, economic and social system of the 1850s as evident on the goldfields, think about the following questions:

Was it right that only those who owned land could vote and enter parliament? Are there certain rights that everyone should have? What makes a good citizen? Should only good citizens have a say in the decision-making process? What makes a good leader? Who has the most say in our school? Why is this so? Should everyone have equal say?

The miners were loyal to Australia.

strongly disagree   strongly agree

0 ... 1 ... 2 ... 3 ... 4 ... 5 ... 6 ... 7 ... 8 ... 9 ... 10

When looking at the Eureka Stockade, think about the following questions: When is violence necessary? Are there real alternatives?

The Eureka Stockade was a waste of lives.

Strongly disagree   strongly agree

0 ... 1 ... 2 ... 3 ... 4 ... 5 ... 6 ... 7 ... 8 ... 9 ... 10

 © 2011 Hawker Brownlow Education • 9781742392547 • HB2547

RESOURCE SHEET

Assignment tasks

1. In any format you like, present the various incidents that led to the ultimate conflict between the authorities and the government. You may choose to present a series of dramatic scenes, such as a wall calendar, ballad, graph or temperature chart of various parties involved in the dispute.

2. After investigating the benefits and disadvantages of the gold licence system, devise a fair system for raising revenue.

3. Raffaello Carboni is suspected of cowardice. After reading his account of the events leading up to the stockade and to the actual battle itself, determine if he deserves this label. Perhaps organise a debate on this topic with other students.

4. Examine the events that led to the battle on 5 December. If you were Peter Lalor, would you have done things differently? Present your decision in any format you wish.

5. Examine the ways in which people that may have previously competed and conflicted with each other cooperated in the battle. Present a graphic organiser that compares what happened in the 1850s to what happens today, in a strike for example.

Chapter 8
Conclusion and evaluation

'No society can long sustain itself unless its members have learned the sensitivities, motivations and skills involved in assisting and caring for other human beings.'

– Urie Bronfenbrenner. (1979) *The Ecology of Human Development: Experiments by Nature and Design.* Cambridge, MA: Harvard University Press, Chapter 3

This chapter provides:

- a rationale for evaluation and assessment.
- a pro forma: Moral reasoning development student profile
- a pro forma: Moral reasoning development class record sheet

This final chapter seeks to bring together the book's diverse elements into a framework for reflecting upon and evaluating students' development of knowledge, skills and dispositions relevant to their moral reasoning ability. A student profile rubric and a class summary assessment sheet are included as a suggested means of recording students' development. These are by no means the only forms of evaluation. Peer assessments in the form of checklists, which ask students to identify each others' strengths, may also generate much useful information. Checklist items could include, for example: 'Who always listens to what you say?', 'Who doesn't use put-downs?' and 'Who says things to keep the discussion focused?'

Ethical development can be seen as being strategic, since the community is most effective when its members can successfully work out how to get along with each other. This book attempts to provide teachers with some strategic tools to use within the curriculum, in order to develop students' ability to identify moral issues, to reason well about moral issues, to make sound moral choices and to communicate effectively within a group.

LaBonte defines the term 'social capital' as:

> Something going on 'out there' in people's day-to-day relationships that is an important determinant to the quality of their lives, if not society's healthy functioning. It is the 'gluey stuff' that binds individuals to groups, groups to organizations, citizens to societies. (1999)

Renzulli applies this term as an imperative of education, stating that:

> Investments in social capital benefit society as a whole because they help to create the values, norms, networks and social trust that facilitate coordination and cooperation geared toward the greater good. (2003)

This book's purpose is to endorse the teaching of affective knowledge, skills and dispositions across the curriculum through ethical discussion and problem-solving, meaningfully linked to subject content.

Children of every age need social skills, because life is communal and building social relationships is integral to communal life. As youngsters, they are taught to follow rules. As children develop, they start to see themselves as individuals, and questions of identity and the nature of relationships arise. They begin to question the rules. For adolescents emerging from a childhood of relative certainties into an adult world of rights, responsibilities and often-conflicting pressures, choosing the right thing to do can be one of their most difficult challenges. In all aspects of adult life, individuals are called upon to make decisions and choices that will impact either positively or negatively upon their own and others' happiness and well-being.

By guiding students through the process of moral reasoning, teachers can help them to make the transition from an orientation towards personal interests to an appreciation of social responsibility, thus facilitating their moral development. Moral reasoning strategies can be taught to students and they can become more skilled at evaluating and justifying moral choices. Whether the development of moral reasoning can generate an increased capacity for higher moral development is a question to be explored more fully in another context.

The strong imperative for teachers is to assist students to make good choices, to want to make good choices and to teach with this aim in mind. It seems that such an essential element of preparation for life is often left to chance and not given specific guidance. Teachers can model moral behaviour. A moral climate can be established in the classroom where reasoning skills can be taught, knowledge of the nature of moral issues can be imparted and practice can be given to encourage the development of cognitive and affective skills and dispositions conducive to making good moral choices.

What knowledge is specific to teaching ethics in the curriculum?

No thinking can be done in a vacuum. Knowledge-poor environments provide little stimulation or fabric for discussion. We advocate that ethics be taught within the curriculum, using the subject content as the context for moral reasoning. Each curriculum area will have its own means of assessing the students' knowledge of the subject content.

In evaluating the level of knowledge that students bring to the moral reasoning process, we suggest that the teacher consider an acceptable standard as one where the student is able to use what they know to help make decisions. A more advanced student would be eager to find out more information and ask questions, or to conduct research in order to expand upon their existing knowledge. The highest level of achievement would be one where the student was able to evaluate all available knowledge and isolate the moral issues involved.

Which skills are critical in ethical decision-making?

There are many skills involved in critical thinking, and many of them are relevant, but there are four skills that the authors have chosen as being of critical importance in teaching ethics through the curriculum.

The first of these is the ability to use the four ethical frameworks or perspectives of principles, agreements, virtues and consequences when making moral choices. At an acceptable level, the students would be able to identify the four perspectives. Being able to apply the four perspectives would achieve a higher standard. The highest level of achievement would indicate that the student could evaluate all four perspectives and select the most appropriate framework to solve a particular moral dilemma.

The second skill is being able to use reasons to justify a position. An acceptable standard would be one where a student can identify the reasons for a position, a higher standard would involve being able to provide reasons for their own position while a more advanced standard would be achieved by the student who can provide the reasoning behind alternative positions. Being able to identify the strengths and weaknesses of a particular idea is another important moral reasoning skill. Some students may accept or reject an idea simply on face value. A higher standard of achievement would be one where the student makes an attempt to identify the idea's strengths and weaknesses, perhaps seeking help to do so, while the student who can apply criteria to identify an idea's strengths and weaknesses would be operating at a high standard of achievement.

Being able to communicate ideas is an essential skill, and the degree to which the student is able to do this may be measured by their enthusiasm and the clarity of their presentation.

What dispositions or attitudes are conducive to moral reasoning?

Renzulli's 'Operation Houndstooth' promotes several dispositions that prompt individuals into choosing to act positively. These are: optimism, courage, romance with a topic or discipline, sensitivity to human concerns, physical and mental energy and vision, and a sense of destiny. Each of these underlying personality factors can help to explain why some people use their abilities in ways that enhance their own and others' well-being and happiness, and why people lacking these traits tend to make poor choices and experience less positive outcomes.

As children interact within their social environment, their personalities and self-concepts are formed. There are many ways in which teachers can nurture the development of positive attitudes and dispositions, and it is hoped that this book may give teachers some insights into how they can construct learning experiences and environments which focus on developing affective strengths. Empathy, active listening, commitment and contribution to the group are some key affective skills which can be used to evaluate moral reasoning ability, and which this book has targeted as learning outcomes.

Final thoughts

Part of our task as teachers is to impart the 'wisdom of the elders' to the students in our care, and to inspire the belief that the ethical life is a worthwhile pursuit. This will empower students with the knowledge, skills and dispositions to make well-informed and reasoned moral choices. As Jane Addams said, 'The good we secure for ourselves is precarious and uncertain until it is secured for all of us and incorporated into our common life.' Active citizenship, where individuals have a voice for themselves and an ear for others' rights within the community, will achieve two very important consequences. Firstly, the individual's development will be enhanced and secondly, the moral fibre of society will be strengthened.

The following evaluation sheets will help tell us if we have achieved these goals.

Moral reasoning development: Student profile

Name _____ Year level _____

INDICATORS	ACCEPTABLE ACHIEVEMENT	GOOD ACHIEVEMENT	OUTSTANDING ACHIEVEMENT
KNOWLEDGE • defining problem	brings own knowledge to help define the problem	finds out more to better understand the problem	isolates the moral issues involved in the problem
SKILLS • using reasons to justify a position	identifies reasons for a position	provides reasons for their own position	provides reasons for alternative position/s
• identifying strengths and weaknesses of an idea	understands that some ideas are better than others	can identify some strengths and weaknesses	applies criteria to identify strengths and weaknesses
• applying four moral frameworks to determine right action	identifies principles, agreements, virtues and consequences	applies four moral frameworks	selects most appropriate framework to apply
• communicating ideas to group	contributes tentative ideas	states ideas clearly	uses enthusiasm, clarity and skill to express ideas
DISPOSITIONS • commitment	committed to the resolution of the moral dilemma	accepts responsibility for resolving dilemma	actively follows through with the group's resolution
• open-mindedness	accepts that their own view may be wrong	willing and able to exchange views	willing to change position if sees justification
• empathy	listens carefully to what others say	can summarise another person's viewpoint	engages others in discussion

Moral reasoning development: Class record sheet

Activity _____

Indicators Students' names	Defines problem	Uses reasons to justify view	Identifies strengths & weaknesses	Applies four moral views	Communicates ideas	Shows commitment	Is open-minded	Shows empathy

 © 2011 Hawker Brownlow Education • 9781742392547 • HB2547

References

Abdelnoor, R.E. J. (1979). *Dominie Mathematical Dictionary.* Brookvale, NSW: Dominie, pp. 21, 30

Applebee, A. N. (1978). *The Child's Concept of Story.* Chicago, Illinois: The University of Chicago Press.

Australian Bureau of Statistics (2003). 3101.0 *Australian Demographic Statistics 11/12/2003. http://www.abs.gov.au/ausstats/abs@.nsf/Lookup/6949409DC8B8FB92CA256BC60001B 3D1,* accessed 06/01/2004

Australian Institute of Criminology. *Juvenile Crime and Justice. http://www.aic.gov.au/ publications/rpp/11/ch2.pdf,* accessed 7 January 2004, p. 28

Bronfenbrenner, Urie. (1979). *The Ecology of Human Development: Experiments by Nature and Design.* Cambridge, MA: Harvard University Press.

Brugman, A. (2002). *Walking Naked.* Crows Nest, NSW: Allen & Unwin.

Bruner, J. (1986). *Actual Minds, Possible Worlds.* Cambridge, USA: Harvard University Press.

Bunting, E. (2000). *Blackwater.* London, England: HarperCollins.

Civic Experts Group (1994). *Whereas the people: civics and citizenship.* Education report of the Civics Expert Group. Canberra, ACT: Australian Government Public Service.

Coerr, E. (1993). *Sadako.* Sydney, NSW: Margaret Hamilton Books.

Crew, G. (1993). *First Light.* South Melbourne, Victoria: Lothian.

Crew, G. (1994). *The Watertower.* Adelaide, South Australia: Era Publications.

Dabrowski, K. (1964). *Positive Disintegration.* Boston, USA: Little, Brown.

de Bono, E. (1998). *Analysing the past – Defining the future.* 40th International Conference of World Education Fellowship, Launceston, Tasmania, Australia

Doherty, B. (1992). *Dear Nobody.* London, United Kingdom: Lions Tracks

Feldhusen, J. F., Van Tassel Baska, J. & Seeley, K. (1989). *Excellence in educating the gifted.* Denver, USA: Love Publishing.

Folsom, C. (1998). 'From a distance: Joining the mind and moral character', *Roeper Review,* Vol. 20 (No. 4).

Gilligan, C. (1982). *In a Different Voice.* Cambridge, USA: Harvard University Press

Gleeson, L. (1998). *Refuge.* Ringwood, Victoria: Penguin

Haddix, M. (2001). *Amongst the Hidden.* London, England: Red Fox Definitions.

Haese, R., Haese, S., Bruce, M., Harris, K., Gaertner-Jones, M., Kappelle, D., Harradine, A., Martin, D. (2001). 'Functions, Statistics and Chance', *Mathematics for Year 11 (Fifth Edition).* Adelaide, South Australia: Haese & Harris Publications, pp. 271, 305

Hinton, S. E. (1972). *The Outsiders.* London, England: Collins.

Innocenti, R. (1985). *Rose Blanche*. London, England: Jonathan Cape.

Jewell, P. D. (1997). 'Debating Policy Issues', *Policy Organisation & Society*. Number 14 (Winter, 1997).

Jewell, P. D. (2000). 'Measuring moral development: Feeling, thinking and doing', *APEX: New Zealand Journal of Gifted Education*, 13.

Jewell, P.D. (2005) 'Autonomy and Liberalism in a multicultural society'. *International Education Journal*, September 2005

Kazemek, F. E. (1986). 'Literature and Moral Development from a Feminine Perspective', *Language Arts*, vol. 63 (3): pp. 264-272.

Kemper, S. (1984). 'The Development of Narrative Skills: Explanations and Entertainment. Discourse Development', *Progress in Cognitive Development Research*. New York, USA: Springer Verlag.

Keyes, D. (1989). *Flowers for Algernon*. Oxford, England: Heinemann.

Kohlberg, L. (1966). *The Psychology of Science*. New York, USA: Harper and Rowe

LaBonte, R. (1999). 'Social capital and community development: Practitioner exemptor', *Australian and New Zealand Journal of Public Health*, 23(4).

Linning, L. (1985). 'Books for Upper Primary Years', *PETA Guide to Children's Literature*. Sydney, NSW: Primary English Teachers Association.

Lowe, I. (1988). *Mathematics at Work Modelling Your World, Vol. 1*. Canberra, ACT: Australian Academy of Science, pp. 42-57

Maker, C. J. (1995). *Teaching Models in Education of the Gifted*. Austin, Texas: PRO-ED.

McFarlane, P. (1996). *The Enemy You Killed*. Ringwood, Victoria: Viking.

Piaget, J. (1965). *Judgement and Reasoning in the Child*. London, England: Routledge and Keegan Paul.

Polkinghorne, D. E. (1988). *Narrative Knowing and the Human Sciences*. New York, USA: State University of New York.

Power, C. N. (1998). *Concepts of a better world in a cross cultural perspective*. 40th International Conference of World Education Fellowship, Launceston, Tasmania, Australia.

Renzulli, J. (2003). 'Conception of giftedness and its relationship to the development of social capital' in N. Colangelo & G. Davis (Eds.), *Handbook of gifted education (3rd edition)*. Boston, USA: Allyn & Bacon.

Rest, J., Narvaez, D., Thoma, S. & Bebeau, M. (2000). 'Neo-Kohlbergian approach to morality research', *Journal of Moral Education*, 29 (No 4), pp. 381–395.

Robinson, D. & Garratt, C. (1996). *Introducing Ethics*. Cambridge, England: Icon Books.

Rogers-Davidson, S. (1999). *Spare Parts*. Ringwood, Victoria: Penguin.

Ruggiero, V. R. (1997). *Thinking Critically About Ethical Issues*. Mountain View, California: Mayfield Publishing Company.

SACSA (2000). *South Australian Curriculum Standards and Accountability Framework, Mathematics*. Adelaide, South Australia: SACSA.

SACSA (2000). *South Australian Curriculum Standards and Accountability Framework, Middle Years Band*. Adelaide, South Australia: SACSA.

Simmonds, J. & Silva, N. (2003). *Maths Zone 8 for South Australia*. Port Melbourne, Victoria: Heinemann, p. 434

SSABSA (2000). *Curriculum Areas* [Online]. Available: Senior Secondary Assessment Board of South Australia (SSABSA).

Stanley, E. (1994). *The Deliverance of Dancing Bears*. Nedlands, Western Australia: Cygnet Books.

Stein, N. L. (1982). 'What's in a Story: An Approach to Comprehension and Instruction', *Advances in Instructional Psychology*, 2 pp. 213–263

Tappan, M. B. (1991). 'Narrative, Language and Moral Experience', *Journal of Moral Education*, 20(3): pp. 243–256

Wagner, W. (1972). *John Brown, Rose and the Midnight Cat*. Harmondsworth, England : Kestrel Books.

Walters, C. (2003). *The Glass Mountain*. St Lucia, Queensland: University of Queensland Press.

Watts, B. (1972). *Mother Holly*. (The Brothers Grimm, retold by Bernadette Watts) New York, USA: North-South Books.

White, K. & Turton, R. (2004). *The Source. www.magpies.net.au*, accessed 16 March 2004.

Winton, T. (1990). *Lockie Leonard Human Torpedo*. Ringwood, Victoria: McPhee Gribble.

Witherell, C. S. (1991). 'Narrative and the Moral Realm: tales of caring and justice', *Journal of Moral Education*, 20(3): pp. 293–303.

Printed in Great Britain
by Amazon